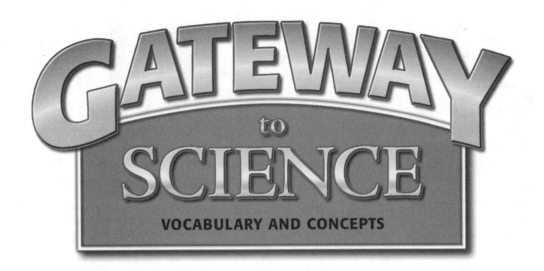

GATEWAY to SCIENCE
VOCABULARY AND CONCEPTS

Tim Collins

Mary Jane Maples

WORKBOOK

HEINLE
CENGAGE Learning

Australia • Brazil • Japan • Korea • Mexico • Singapore • Spain • United Kingdom • United States

HEINLE
CENGAGE Learning

Gateway to Science Workbook
Tim Collins, Mary Jane Maples

Publisher, School ESL: Sherrise Roehr

VP, Director of Content Development:
  Anita Raducanu

Senior Development Editor: Guy de Villiers

Executive Marketing Manager:
  Jim McDonough

Director of Product Marketing: Amy Mabley

Associate Production Editor:
  John Sarantakis

Print Buyer: Susan Carroll

Project Management, Design,
and Composition:
  InContext Publishing Partners

Cover Designer: Chrome Media/InContext
  Publishing Partners

ISBN-13: 978-1-4240-0332-7

ISBN-10: 1-4240-0332-6

Heinle
25 Thomson Place
Boston, MA 02210
USA

Cengage Learning is a leading provider of customized learning solutions with office locations around the globe, including Singapore, the United Kingdom, Australia, Mexico, Brazil and Japan. Locate our local office at: **international.cengage.com/region**

Cengage Learning products are represented in Canada by Nelson Education, Ltd.

Visit Heinle online at **elt.heinle.com**
Visit our corporate website at **cengage.com**

Printed in Canada
2 3 4 5 6 7 8 9 10   11 10 09 08

CONTENTS

Ⓐ VOCABULARY WORDS

Match the items on the left with the correct definitions.

Example: 9. conclusion   __9__ the plant died because it didn't get enough sun

1. correlational design   ____ describing a plant in a garden

2. observation   ____ breaking a toy apart to see how it works

3. question   ____ the belief that a plant will die without sun

4. hypothesis   ____ testing to see if too much water kills a plant

5. prediction   ____ asking how rainbows happen

6. descriptive design   ____ predicting that a dog will eat beef but not fish

7. data   ____ watching birds build a nest

8. analyze   ____ the seeds were planted two weeks ago

Ⓑ VOCABULARY IN CONTEXT

Choose words from the box to complete the paragraph.

analyze	conclusion	experimental design	hypothesis
observation	prediction	question	~~experiment~~

Example: You can test a hypothesis by doing an ___experiment___.

Ana's computer screen was blank. She asked her brother a(n)

(1) _____: Why doesn't the screen work? They decided to use

a(n) (2) _____ to solve the problem. First, Ana made the

(3) _____ that the light on the monitor was not blinking.

Using this data, she formed a(n) (4) _____. She believed that it

was not blinking because the monitor was not getting power. They began to

(5) _____ the monitor. They checked the switch and the

power cord. They found that the plug was not in the wall. Ana made a(n)

(6) _____ that if she plugged it back in, the light would blink. They

made the (7) _____ that the monitor must be plugged in to work.

📖 Student book pages 4–5

C OBSERVING AND DESCRIBING

Reading Strategy *Comparing and Contrasting*

Read **Observing and Describing** on page 4 of your student book. Then answer the questions below.

> **Comparing and Contrasting**
> ✓ Tell how things are the same (compare).
> ✓ Tell how things are different (contrast).

1. What is the same about the food that hummingbirds and sparrows eat?

   _____

2. What is the same about the food that hummingbirds and woodpeckers eat?

   _____

3. What is different about the food that warblers and sparrows eat?

   _____

D FINDING RELATIONSHIPS

Reading Strategy *Inferring from Evidence*

Read the information in the chart. Then think where you might find the three types of birds. Answer the questions.

> **Inferring from Evidence**
> ✓ Make a guess about something from facts that you know.

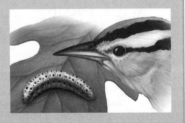

| Woodpeckers have long, sharp beaks for drilling into wood to get insects, such as termites and ants. | Hummingbirds have long, thin beaks for reaching nectar in flowers. | Warblers have thin, pointed beaks for catching caterpillars and flying insects. |

Example: Where do you think woodpeckers live? <u>Woodpeckers have beaks for drilling into wood. You might find them in a forest.</u>

1. Where do you think hummingbirds live? _____

   _____

2. Where do you think warblers live? _____

   _____

E SCIENCE SKILL Looking at Relationships

Think about the types of foods babies eat and the foods adults eat. How are they different? What things affect which foods babies and adults eat? Complete the chart below.

> **Looking at Relationships**
> ✓ When you look at relationships, you look at how one thing affects another thing.

	Babies	Adults
What do they eat?	1.	3.
What things affect what they eat?	2. no teeth	4.

F EXPERIMENTING

Pairwork

Read **Experimenting** on page 5 of your student book. Prepare questions and answers about the information. Then ask your partner the questions.

Example: Question: Which insulation material kept the ice frozen for the shortest time?

Answer: Bubble wrap kept ice frozen the shortest time.

1. Question: _____

   Answer: _____

2. Question: _____

   Answer: _____

G WRITING Hypothesizing

Which do you think would sink faster in a bowl of water, a hard-boiled egg or a raw egg? Describe how you could use one of the scientific methods to find the answer. Write a paragraph.

> **Hypothesizing**
> ✓ Tell what you think will happen.
> ✓ Give reasons to support your idea.

_____

_____

_____

_____

LAB **Group Work** Paper Airplanes

Question Does material affect how far a paper airplane will fly?

Procedure

1. With your group, make a paper airplane out of each type of paper. Be sure to make each one the same way.
2. Predict which airplane will fly the farthest. Predict which one will fly the shortest distance.

_____

_____

Materials
- construction paper
- notebook paper
- tracing paper
- meter stick or measuring tape

3. Choose one person from your group to throw the airplanes. Standing in the same place, the thrower should throw each of the airplanes. Use the same amount of force for each throw.
4. Measure how far each airplane flew. Record your data in the table.

Material	How far did it fly?
Construction paper	
Notebook paper	
Tracing paper	

Analysis

1. **Compare** your prediction with the data from the table. Were your predictions correct or incorrect?

_____

2. Which material flew the longest distance? Which flew the shortest distance?

_____

3. **Draw a conclusion.** Does material affect how far a paper airplane can fly?

_____

_____

Name _____ Date _____

A VOCABULARY WORDS

Circle the word or words that complete each sentence.

Example: A (thermometer) / beaker is a tool that measures temperature.

1. You can use a telescope / microscope to look at stars.

2. Scientists can store information in a petri dish / computer.

3. Scientists can use anemometers / test tubes to hold things they are testing.

Use each word that you did not circle in a sentence.

Example: _A beaker measures liquids._

4. _____

5. _____

6. _____

B VOCABULARY IN CONTEXT

Choose words from the box to complete the paragraph.

| beaker | test tube | computer | telescope | ~~graduated cylinder~~ |
| balance | anemometer | thermometer | microscope | |

Example: Scientists can use a _graduated cylinder_ to measure volume.

Scientists need many kinds of tools. They use some tools to measure things.
A(n) (1) _____ measures temperature. Wind speeds can be
measured using a(n) (2) _____. A(n) (3) _____ could
be used to measure an amount of liquid. A(n) (4) _____ can be
used to compare masses. Sometimes scientists use tools to store things. They might
store a substance to be tested in a(n) (5) _____. Measurements
and test results could be stored in a(n) (6) _____. Some tools help
scientists look closely at things. A(n) (7) _____ makes very small
things appear bigger, and a(n) (8) _____ makes far away objects
appear closer.

📖 Student book pages 8–9

C FINDING VOLUME BY DISPLACEMENT

Reading Strategy *Sequencing*

Read the paragraph. Then use numbers 1–6 to put the steps below the paragraph in the correct order.

First choose an object whose volume you want to measure. Next fill a graduated cylinder about half full of water. Record the volume of water. Drop your object into the water. Record the new volume. Finally, subtract the first reading from the second reading. The answer is the volume of your object.

_____ Drop the object into the water.

_____ Fill a graduated cylinder about half full of water.

_____ Record the volume of only the water.

_____ Choose an object to measure.

_____ Record the volume of the water and the object.

_____ Subtract the volume of the water from the volume of the water and the object.

Sequencing

✓ Sequence tells you the order in which things happen.

✓ Words like <u>first</u> and <u>next</u> help explain the sequence of something.

D A COMPOUND MICROSCOPE

Reading Strategy *Scanning for Information*

Read questions 1–3 below. Then read **A Compound Microscope** on page 8 of your student book and find the answers.

Scanning for Information

✓ Understand the information you need before reading.

✓ Read to find the information.

1. Where do you place the object you want to see?	
2. What does the eyepiece lens do?	
3. How do you make the object on the slide look clear?	

E **SCIENCE SKILL** **Reading Volume on a Graduated Cylinder**

Read the numbers from the bottom of the meniscus to find the volume of water in each graduated cylinder. Answer the questions.

1. What is the water volume in cylinder A?

   _____

2. What is the water volume in cylinder B?

   _____

3. What is the volume of the rock?

   _____

Reading Volume on a Graduated Cylinder

✓ Volume is the amount of space a solid, liquid, or gas takes up. The markings on a graduated cylinder measure the volume of liquid in the container. The meniscus is the curved line made by the water.

A.
- 50 mL
- 45
- 40
- 35
- 30
- 25
- 20
- 15
- 10
- 5

B.
- 50 mL
- 45
- 40
- 35
- 30
- 25
- 20
- 15
- 10
- 5

F **GOES WEATHER SATELLITE**

Pairwork

Work with a partner. Use the internet to find out more about the GOES Weather Satellite. When was the first GOES launched? How high are they above Earth? Who uses the information provided by GOES satellites? Write your answers.

_____

_____

_____

G **WRITING** **Applying Information**

How do science tools help scientists with their jobs? Write a paragraph.

Applying Information

✓ Use information for a particular reason.

_____

_____

_____

LAB Group Work Mass

Question How does the mass of an object compare to the mass of its parts?

Procedure
1. With your group, build something out of your blocks.
2. Use a balance to **measure** the mass of your structure. Record the mass in the table.

Materials
- large plastic building blocks
- balance

Structure	Mass of structure	Length of structure	Total mass of parts
1			
2			
3			
4			

3. Measure the length of the longest side of your structure. Record this length in the table.
4. Now take your structure apart. Measure the mass of each part. Add the masses of the parts together. Record this total in the table.
5. Do steps 1–4 three more times, making a different structure each time. Use the same blocks each time.

Analysis
1. How did the mass of each structure **compare** to the total mass of its parts?

_____

_____

2. How did the masses of structures 1, 2, 3, and 4 **compare** to their lengths?

_____

_____

Name _____ Date _____

A VOCABULARY WORDS

Match the items on the left with the correct definitions.

Example: 10. degrees Celsius   <u>10</u> measurement of temperature (C)

1. milliliter   _____ the base unit for length (m)

2. liter   _____ one thousand grams (kg)

3. meter   _____ the base unit for mass (g)

4. centimeter   _____ one thousandth of a liter (mL)

5. millimeter   _____ the volume of a cube 1 cm on each side (cm^3)

6. kilometer   _____ one hundredth of a meter (cm)

7. cubic centimeter   _____ one thousand meters (km)

8. kilogram   _____ one thousandth of a meter (mm)

9. gram   _____ the base unit for volume (L)

B VOCABULARY IN CONTEXT

Choose words from the box to complete the paragraphs.

centimeter	degrees Celsius	gram	liter
~~length~~	millimeter	kilometer	

Example: The metric system uses the meter to measure _____ length _____.

The meter is the base unit. Imagine you have a piece of string that is one meter long. If you cut it into one hundred pieces, each piece would be one

(1) _____. If you cut it into one thousand pieces, each piece would

be one (2) _____. Now, imagine you have one thousand pieces

of string that are each one meter long. If you put them together end to end, your

string is one thousand meters long, or one (3) _____.

To measure liquids, the metric system uses the (4) _____. To

measure mass, it uses the (5) _____. To measure temperature, the

metric system uses (6) _____.

📖 Student book pages 12–13

C THE METRIC SYSTEM

Reading Strategy *Summarizing*

Read **The Metric System** on page 12 of your book.
Write a summary below.

> **Summarizing**
> ✓ Write something in a shorter form.

_____

_____

_____

_____

_____

D TEMPERATURE SCALES

Reading Strategy *Using Math*

Read these steps to change the temperature
from degrees Fahrenheit to degrees Celsius.
Then convert the city temperatures in the table to
degrees Celsius.

> **Using Math**
> ✓ Use math to convert data from one measurement system to another measurement system.

1. Subtract 32 from the number in the chart.

2. Divide the answer by 9.

3. Multiply that number by 5.

City	Fahrenheit temperature on March 17, 2007	Celsius temperature on March 17, 2007
Boston, USA	30°F	
Mexico City, Mexico	68°F	
Montreal, Canada	23°F	

E SCIENCE SKILL Comparing and Contrasting

Use the units of measurement listed in the box to answer the questions.

| centimeter | kilometer | liter |
| meter | milliliter | millimeter |

1. Which units measure volume? _____

2. Which units measure distance? _____

3. Which distance unit is also a basic unit of measurement? _____

4. Which volume unit is also a basic unit of measurement? _____

F THE METRIC SYSTEM

Pairwork

With a partner, read aloud each of the questions in the chart below. Complete the chart with the unit of measurement you would use and tell why.

How do you measure . . .	I would measure in . . .
how heavy you are?	kilograms because it is mass.
how much water is in a bucket?	1.
how long our classroom is?	2.

G WRITING Analyzing Information

Most of the world uses the metric system. The United States uses other measurements. Why is it easier to change centimeters to meters than to change inches to feet? Write a paragraph.

_____

_____

_____

_____

LAB **Group Work** Estimating

Question How well can you estimate length and mass?

Procedure

1. Choose three small objects in the classroom. Write the names of the objects on index cards.
2. Measure the length and mass of each object. Write the length and mass of each object on its card.
3. A student draws a card and tries to find a classroom object the same length without measuring.
4. Another person from the group measures the object and records the lengths of both objects in the table below.
5. Use numbers to find the difference between the two lengths.

Materials
- pencil
- metric ruler
- balance
- objects to measure
- index cards

Length of object on card (in cm)	Length of classroom object (in cm)	Difference

6. After length, repeat the game using the mass of each object.

Mass of object on card (in grams)	Mass of classroom object (in grams)	Difference

Analysis

1. **Interpret your data.** Which trial produced the smallest difference? Which produced the largest difference?

_____

_____

2. How would you change this activity to estimate the volume of different cups of water?

_____

_____

📖 Student book pages 14–15

A VOCABULARY WORDS

Match the items on the left with the correct definition.

Example: 7. line graph ___7___ data is shown by points and lines

1. map   _____ a diagram that shows steps in a process

2. pie chart   _____ a chart showing data in numbers and words

3. flowchart   _____ a diagram that uses circles to show how two things are alike and different

4. Venn diagram   _____ a circle divided into sections to show the parts of something

5. data table

6. map key   _____ a drawing of a particular area, such as a country

                  _____ a list that explains the meanings of symbols on a map

B VOCABULARY IN CONTEXT

Choose words from the box to complete the paragraph.

line graph	Venn diagram	bar graph
pie chart	map	flowchart

Example: If you wanted to show the percent of electricity made from different

fuels, you could use a _____pie chart_____.

There are many ways to present data or information. If you need to show how

two things are alike and different, you could use a (1) _____. If you

need to show the order of a process, you could use a (2) _____.

Sometimes you must show how information changes over time. Suppose you must

show how a child's height changes from year to year. For this you could use a

(3) _____ or a (4) _____. To show information about

a city, you could use a (5) _____.

C UNDERSTANDING TABLES

Reading Strategy *Transferring Information*

Read the information below. Then transfer the information to the table.

> **Transferring Information**
> ✓ Transfer data to a table to compare the data more easily.

January was a cold month. The average temperature was 9°C. February was a little warmer. The average temperature was three degrees higher than January. March was just one degree warmer than February. The average temperature in April was 15°C.

Average Monthly Temperatures	
Month	**Temperature (°C)**

D UNDERSTANDING GRAPHS

Reading Strategy *Drawing Conclusions*

Look at the bar graph showing the average rainfall in Union County, PA. Use it to answer the question.

> **Drawing Conclusions**
> ✓ Make a decision after you think about all the facts.

Average Rainfall in Union County, PA

What conclusion can you draw about the weather in Union County in the summer? Why?

_____

_____

E **SCIENCE SKILL** Organizing Data

The Cougars are a basketball team. The team keeps track of what each player does. The team records how many points each player scores. It also records how many rebounds each player gets. Use the data table to answer the questions.

Organizing Data
✓ A data table helps you organize and understand information.

Cougars vs. Sharks, April 7		
Player	**Points Scored**	**Rebounds**
Jill	25	5
Teresa	16	9
Barbara	7	14
Maria	15	2
Sue	12	8

1. Which players had more than 7 rebounds? _____

    _____

2. Which player scored the fewest points? _____

3. How many more points did Jill score than Maria? _____

F **UNDERSTANDING PIE CHARTS**

Pairwork

Work with a partner. Ask each classmate what his or her favorite color is. Record the information. Then make a pie chart to show your results.

G **WRITING** Applying Information

How are charts and tables helpful to scientists? Write a paragraph.

Applying Information
✓ Use information for a particular reason.

_____

_____

_____

_____

LAB **Group Work** Pet Graphs

Question How can you organize data?

Procedure

1. Conduct a class survey. Ask each classmate, "What kinds of pets do you have?" Write down each person's response.
2. Organize the data in a tally chart like the one below. First write down each type of pet. For example, if a classmate has a bird, write *bird* in the chart. Then add a tally mark. Add a tally mark by *bird* each time someone says they have a bird. Do this for each pet.

Materials
- notebook
- pen or pencil
- graph paper

Kinds of Pets	
Dog	IIII
Cat	II
Bird	II
Fish	III

3. Count up the tallies to find the total for each pet.
4. Now make a bar graph of the data. Study the bar graph on page 16 of your textbook. A bar graph has numbers on the side. It has words across the bottom. Make your graph with graph paper. Write numbers along the side of your graph. Write the names of the kinds of pets across the bottom of the graph.
5. Make a bar for each kind of pet. Start at the bottom and fill in one box for each tally mark.
6. Give your graph a title. Write the title at the top of the graph.

Analysis

1. **Interpret the data.** Which pet is the most popular? Which pet is the least popular?

   _____

   _____

2. What are some other ways you could show the pet data you collected?

   _____

   _____

Data Analysis • LAB

SCIENCE BASICS

Name _____   Date _____

A VOCABULARY WORDS

Write a definition for each item in the chart.

goggles	special glasses that protect your eyes
lab apron	**1.**
gloves	**2.**
soap and water	**3.**
fire extinguisher	**4.**
fire alarm	**5.**
first aid kit	**6.**

B VOCABULARY IN CONTEXT

Choose words from the box to complete the paragraph.

fire extinguisher	goggles	fire alarm	~~first aid kit~~
lab apron	soap and water	gloves	

Example: If you get a cut, your teacher will use the ___first aid kit___.

It is important to stay safe while in the science lab. Be sure to follow all of the lab safety rules and use the proper safety equipment. For example, you should always wear your safety (1) _____. These will protect your eyes. You should wear a (2) _____. This can protect your body. (3) _____ will protect your hands. If you accidentally get a chemical on you, wash the area with (4) _____. If a fire accidentally starts, you or your teacher should put it out with a (5) _____. If the fire is large, pull the (6) _____ in your classroom.

SCIENCE BASICS · Safety in the Lab · **CONCEPTS**

C STAYING SAFE

Reading Strategy *Main Idea and Details*

Read **Staying Safe** on page 20 of your student book. Write the main idea in the top box. Write one detail in each box.

> **Main Idea and Details**
> ✓ The main idea of a paragraph is the big idea.
> ✓ Details support the main idea.

Main Idea:			
Detail Avoid injuries by wearing goggles, gloves, and a lab apron.	**Detail**	**Detail**	**Detail**

D RESPONDING TO ACCIDENTS

Reading Strategy *Problem and Solution*

Read the paragraph. Use it to complete the chart.

> **Problem and Solution**
> ✓ A problem is a difficult situation.
> ✓ A solution solves the problem.

James, Luisa, and Kim had to study a chemical powder. They poured some of the powder into a glass dish. James coughed while observing the powder. Some of the powder blew out of the dish and onto the table. The students carefully brushed the powder back into the dish. But Luisa was not wearing her gloves. She accidentally touched the powder, so she washed her hands with soap and water. Later, the students were putting the powder on a glass slide. Kim accidentally cut his finger on the slide's sharp corner. His teacher took out the first aid kit. He cleaned and bandaged Kim's cut.

Problem	Solution
The students spilled the powder.	The students brushed the powder back into the dish.
Luisa touched the powder.	1.
Kim cut his finger.	2.

E SCIENCE SKILL Reading Safety Signs and Warnings

Some safety and warning signs use words. Others use pictures. Some use both words and pictures. Match the words in the box to the safety signs.

> **Reading Safety Signs and Warnings**
> ✓ A safety sign shows people how to be safe. A warning sign warns people of possible danger.

| hand washing | safety goggles | lab apron | animal safety |

1. _____

2. _____

3. _____

4. _____

F TREATMENT OF LIVING THINGS

Pairwork

Scientists often study plants, animals, and other living things. It is important not to harm living things in lab work or outside of class. Think how you can study living things without disturbing nature. Make a list with your partner.

Example: We can take photos of living things. _____

1. _____

2. _____

3. _____

G WRITING Making Observations

Imagine you are in a very safe science lab. What things do you observe in the lab that tell you it is safe? Write a paragraph.

> **Making Observations**
> ✓ Look at something closely to learn about it.

_____

_____

_____

_____

LAB **Group Work** Safety and Reactions

Question Are you being safe?

Procedure

1. Sometimes a chemical change happens when two substances are mixed together. The chemical change may produce heat, bubbles, or a change of color.

2. Put on your safety goggles, gloves, and lab apron. Why do you think you might need these for this experiment?

_____

_____

3. Pour 5 mL of water into a cup. Then put a spoonful of baking soda into the cup. Stir the baking soda into the water. What steps did you take to do this safely?

_____

4. Observe what happens when the baking soda mixes with the water. Describe what you see.

_____

5. Pour 5 mL of vinegar into a cup. Then put a spoonful of baking soda into the cup. Stir the baking soda into the vinegar.

6. Observe what happens when the baking soda mixes with the vinegar. Describe what you see.

_____

> **Materials**
> - 2 beakers or clear plastic cups
> - water
> - vinegar
> - baking soda
> - plastic spoon
> - 10-mL graduated cylinder

Analysis

1. What did you do during this experiment to keep yourself safe?

_____

_____

2. Which substance produced a chemical change when mixed with baking soda? How could you tell that a change took place?

_____

_____

A VOCABULARY WORDS

Label the parts of the cell.

Plant cell

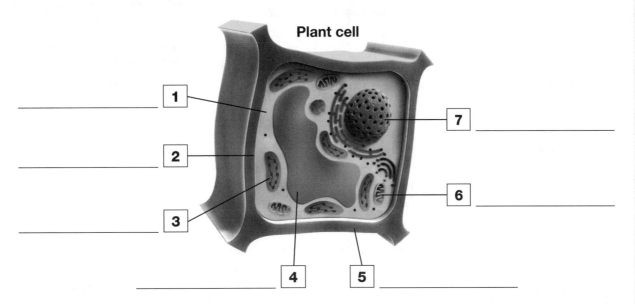

_____ 1

_____ 2

_____ 3

_____ 4   5 _____

7 _____

6 _____

B VOCABULARY IN CONTEXT

Choose words from the box to complete the paragraphs.

cell membrane	chloroplasts	~~vacuoles~~	nucleus
cytoplasm	cells	cell wall	mitochondria
lysosomes	ribosomes		

Example: _____Vacuoles_____ store water, food, and waste.

Living things are made up of (1) _____. Inside every

cell is a jelly-like material called (2) _____. All cells have

a (3) _____ around the cytoplasm. Plants cells have a

(4) _____ outside the membrane.

Each cell part has a job. In plant and animal cells, the (5) _____

controls how the cell works. Proteins are made on (6) _____.

(7) _____ break down materials. Cells get energy as

(8) _____ act on food. In plants, (9) _____ make

food from sunlight.

C WHAT DO ORGANELLES DO?

Reading Strategy *Scanning for Information*

Read questions 1–3 below. Then read **What Do Organelles Do?** on page 24 of your student book and find the answers.

> **Scanning for Information**
> ✓ Understand what information you need before reading.
> ✓ Read to find the information.

1. Which organelles do animal cells not have?

   _____

2. Where is the cytoplasm in the cell? _____

   _____

3. What does the cell wall do? _____

   _____

D ROBERT HOOKE SEES CELLS

Reading Strategy *Cause and Effect*

Read **Robert Hooke Sees Cells** on page 24 in your student book. Look at the pictures in the Word Study on page 22. Then answer the questions.

> **Cause and Effect**
> ✓ The cause tells what happened.
> ✓ The effect is the result of the cause.

1. *Cause*

   a. What did Hooke see under the microscope?

   _____

   _____

   b. Which picture in the Word Study did they look like?

   _____

   _____

2. *Effect* What did Hooke name the things he saw?

   _____

   _____

   _____

   _____

Hooke's drawing of cork cells

E SCIENCE SKILL Reading a Table

Cells are not all alike. Plant cells are different from animal cells. In the table below, the left column lists cell parts. The middle column tells if the part is in plant cells. The right column tells if the part is in animal cells. Use the table to answer the questions.

1. What cell parts are missing from animal cells?

   _____

   _____

2. What cell parts are in both plant cells and animal cells?

   _____

   _____

How Plant and Animal Cells Differ		
Cell Parts	**Plant Cells**	**Animal Cells**
cell wall	yes	no
cell membrane	yes	yes
cytoplasm	yes	yes
chloroplasts	yes	no
nucleus	yes	yes
mitochondria	yes	yes
vacuoles	one large	many small

3. How are vacuoles in plant cells and vacuoles in animal cells different?

   _____

   _____

F BACTERIA CELLS

Pairwork

Read about bacteria cells on page 25 in your student book. Talk about bacteria cells with a partner. How are they the same as other cells? How are they different?

G WRITING Integrating Information

Why are cells important? Write a paragraph.

_____

_____

_____

_____

_____

_____

LAB Group Work Modeling Cells

Question How can you make a model of a plant cell and an animal cell?

Procedure

1. Use scissors to cut the gray construction paper into two pieces (12 cm x 10 cm). Glue each to the poster board as the cytoplasm for the plant cell and the animal cell.
2. Use a marker. Label one cell *Plant Cell.* Label the other cell *Animal Cell.*
3. Cut two 3-cm circles from the orange paper. Use one to make a model of the nucleus of the plant cell. Use the other orange circle for the nucleus of the animal cell.

   Safety Note: *Adult help needed. Wait for your teacher to cut paper and yarn.*

Materials	• metric ruler
• poster board	• blue yarn
• green construction paper	• split peas
	• dried lima beans
• orange construction paper	• glue
	• scissors
• light gray construction paper	• small plastic sandwich bag
• 6 rubber bands	• crayons or markers
	• 8 foam packing pieces

4. Cut 4 strips of green paper, each 1 cm wide, to make the plant cell wall.
5. Write a cell part for each material you will use in the models.

   a. rubber bands _____   **f.** dried lima beans _____

   b. foam packing pieces _____   **g.** gray paper _____

   c. small sandwich bag _____   **h.** orange paper _____

   d. blue yarn _____   **i.** green paper _____

   e. split peas _____

6. Glue the materials in place on the plant cell. Do the same for the animal cell.
7. Use a crayon to draw the small vacuoles in the animal cell. Use a different color to draw lysosomes in each cell.
8. Label each part of the plant cell. Label each part of the animal cell.

Analysis

1. How can a **model** help you learn the parts of a cell? _____

   _____

2. How are your **models** alike and different? Write your **conclusion.**

   _____

   _____

Gateway to Science Workbook • Copyright © Heinle, Cengage Learning

A VOCABULARY WORDS

Circle the word or words that complete each sentence.

Example: (Flagella) / Pseudopods are long whip-like cell parts.

1. People use single-celled organisms called yeast / bacteria to make bread.

2. An amoeba uses its flagella / pseudopods to move and get food.

3. Yeast is one kind of fungus / algae.

4. Bacteria / Paramecium can be rod, round, or spiral in shape.

5. Some one-celled organisms use hairlike cilia / dinoflagellates to move.

6. Some fungi / algae use sunlight to make their own food.

B VOCABULARY IN CONTEXT

Choose words from the box to complete the paragraph.

cilia	bacteria	pseudopod	fungus	~~trichonympha~~
dinoflagellates	yeast	flagellum	algae	

Example: ___Trichonympha___ is a protozoan that feeds on wood pieces inside termites.

One-celled organisms obtain food in a variety of ways. Amoebas send

out a false foot called a(n) (1) _____ that surrounds food.

Paramecia move through water by beating tiny hair-like (2) _____.

Euglena and (3) _____ wave a whip-like cell part called a(n)

(4) _____. Many (5) _____ contain chlorophyll.

They can make their own food. Some foods that humans eat have

(6) _____ or bacteria in them. Yeast is a(n) (7) _____

that makes bread rise. To make cheese and yogurt, you need

(8) _____.

C KINDS OF SINGLE-CELLED ORGANISMS

Reading Strategy *Cause and Effect*

Read **Kinds of Single-Celled Organisms** on page 28 in your student book. Complete the chart. Read the cause in the left column. Then write the effect in the right column.

> **Cause and Effect**
> ✓ The cause tells what happened.
> ✓ The effect is the result of the cause.

Cause ➡	Effect
Sunlight shines on an euglena.	1.
No sunlight shines on an euglena.	2.
An amoeba forms pseudopods.	3.

D GETTING ENERGY

Reading Strategy *Inferring from Evidence*

Read **Getting Energy** on page 28 in your student book. What must algae contain in order to make food from sunlight? Explain your answer.

> **Inferring from Evidence**
> ✓ Make a guess about something from facts you know.

_____

_____

_____

_____

E SCIENCE SKILL Comparing and Contrasting

Read the passage and look at the pictures. Then answer the questions.

Single-celled organisms can be grouped or classified by how they move. Some are covered with many short cilia. Cilia move back and forth. They move the organism through the water. They also stir up food that it can feed on. Flagella look like long tails. They move back and forth. They also cause food to flow around the organism so that it can scoop food up. Some one-celled organisms have neither cilia nor flagella.

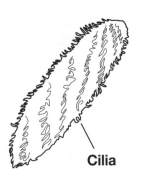

Cilia   **Flagella**

1. How are cilia different from flagella? Name two ways. _____

_____

2. What are two things that are the same about cilia and flagella? _____

_____

F EXTREME CONDITIONS FOR LIFE

Pairwork

Work with a partner. Look in library books or on the internet. Learn about the bacteria and algae in Great Salt Lake. Find out the answers to the following questions. (1) How is Great Salt Lake different from other lakes? (2) How are the bacteria and algae in Great Salt Lake important to other things that live there? (3) How do the northern and southern parts of the lake differ? (4) How do living things in the two parts of the lake differ? Make a list of the information you find.

G WRITING Comparing and Contrasting

Compare and contrast how amoebas get food with the way green algae get their food. Tell how they are the same and different. Write a paragraph.

_____

_____

_____

LAB **Group Work** Model Single-Celled Organisms

Question What can you learn about single-celled organisms by making models?

Procedure
1. Choose two different single-celled organisms to model. Look at pages 26, 27, and 28 of your student book. Write the names of the organisms:

   a. _____

   b. _____

2. Decide what materials to use to make your models.
3. Make your model. Mount it on a sheet of construction paper.

   Safety Note: Be careful when working with scissors.

4. Write the name of each organism you modeled. Use index cards. Tell one fact about each one. Write a sentence on each card.

Materials
- construction paper
- clay
- markers
- scissors
- feathers
- glue
- yarn
- index cards

Analysis
1. How are your two models different from each other? _____

   _____

   _____

   _____

2. What can your models teach you about single-celled organisms?

   _____

   _____

   _____

A VOCABULARY WORDS

Label the picture of the respiratory system.

| organ | cell | organ system | tissue |

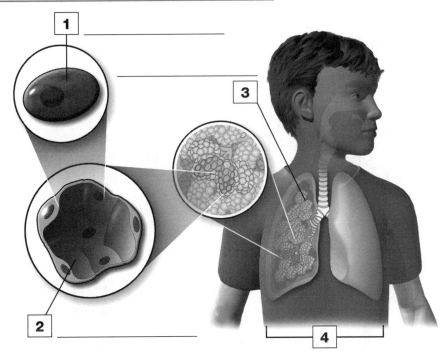

1 _____

2 _____

3

4

_____

B VOCABULARY IN CONTEXT

Choose words from the box to complete the paragraph.

| multicellular | organ | ~~cell~~ | organ system | tissue |

Example: Many living things are made up of more than one _____*cell*_____.

Living things made of many cells are called (1) _____ organisms.
They are organized in a predictable way. Groups of the same kind of cell are called

(2) _____. They do the same kind of work. For example, cells in

plant stems form tubes that carry water. Two or more tissues work together to form

a(n) (3) _____. A leaf is an example. When many such structures

work together, they form a(n) (4) _____. The plant's shoot system is

an example.

C **KINDS OF ANIMAL CELLS**

Reading Strategy *Integrating Information*

Study the table under **Kinds of Animal Cells** on page 32 in your student book. Then read the paragraph below. Use the table and the reading to answer the question.

> **Integrating Information**
> ✓ When you integrate information, you bring together parts to make a whole idea.

    Our circulatory system is made up of blood, blood vessels, and the heart. When the heart beats, it pushes blood through tubes called blood vessels. Blood vessels are found in the heart and in the rest of the body.

What kinds of cells form the tissues and organs in your circulatory system?

_____

_____

D **HOW CELLS DIVIDE**

Reading Strategy *Asking Questions*

Read **How Cells Divide** on page 33 of your student book. Write questions and answers about the reading to check your understanding.

> **Asking Questions**
> ✓ When you read, ask yourself questions to check your understanding.
> ✓ Use words like <u>what</u>, <u>where</u>, <u>when</u>, <u>why</u>, and <u>how</u> to form questions.

Questions	Answers
What is cell division?	the way cells make new cells

E SCIENCE SKILL Looking for Details

Read the table on page 32 of your student book. Then look for the details that answer the questions.

1. What kind of cell carries gases to other cells in the body?

   _____

2. What kind of cell lines the blood vessels and airways of the lungs?

   _____

3. What kind of cell hunts and eats germs and bacteria? _____

4. What kind of cell supports your body and also helps you move?

   _____

F HOW CELLS DIVIDE

Pairwork

Work with a partner. Look at the drawing of cell division on page 33 in your student book. Make a model of how a cell divides. Work together to decide what materials to use for the model. Write your ideas below. Then make the model. Explain your model to the class.

_____

_____

_____

G WRITING Applying Information

Explain how cells in a multicellular organism fit together. Use an example such as breathing or the shoots of a tree. Write a paragraph.

_____

_____

_____

_____

LAB **Group Work** Observing Plant Cells and Tissues

Question How are tissues from different parts of a plant alike and different?

Procedure

1. Place the slide of the plant root on the microscope stage. Use the knob to focus the image. You should see the cells clearly.
2. Observe the cells and the tissue they make. Using your colored pencils, draw what you see in the box below.
3. Repeat Steps 1 and 2. Draw the plant stem and the plant leaf.

Materials
- prepared slides of a plant root, a plant stem, and a plant leaf
- microscope
- paper
- colored pencils

Plant Root	Plant Stem	Plant Leaf

4. Compare and contrast your drawings. How are the tissues from the three plant parts alike? How are they different?

_____

_____

Analysis

1. When you infer, you use what you know to reach a conclusion. In plants, food is made in the leaves. Use this information to **make an inference** about why leaves are green.

_____

_____

Name _____ Date _____

📖 Student book pages 34–35

A VOCABULARY WORDS

Label the plant drawing.

_____ 1

_____ 2

_____ 3

_____ 4

B VOCABULARY IN CONTEXT

Choose words from the box to complete the paragraph.

~~sunlight~~	soil	fruits	cones
seeds	spores	leaves	roots

Example: All plants need energy from _____sunlight_____.

Plant (1) _____ use energy from sunlight to make food. Plant

(2) _____ take in water from the (3) _____.

Soil gives the plant materials it needs to build its parts. Plants can use either

(4) _____ or (5) _____ to reproduce. Plants that

make seeds have different ways to hold and spread them. Some hold seeds

in tasty (6) _____ and still others store their seeds in hard

(7) _____.

📖 Student book pages 36–37

C **PLANT PARTS**

Reading Strategy *Main Idea and Details*

Read the second paragraph of **Plant Parts** on page 36 of your student book. Then complete the chart with details that support the main idea.

Main Idea and Details

✓ The main idea of a paragraph is the big idea.

✓ Details support the main idea.

Main Idea: Roots do many jobs for plants.		
Detail	**Detail**	**Detail**

D **WHAT IS SOIL?**

Reading Strategy *Asking Questions*

Read **What Is Soil?** on page 36 of your student book. Write questions and answers about the reading to check your understanding.

Asking Questions

✓ When you read, ask yourself questions to check your understanding.

✓ Use words like <u>what</u>, <u>where</u>, <u>when</u>, <u>why</u>, and <u>how</u> to form questions.

Questions	Answers
What is soil?	Soil is a mixture of rock, humus, air, and water.

Name _____   Date _____

E SCIENCE SKILL Reading Bar Graphs

A student collected three samples of soil and made
a bar graph to show how much of each soil is made
of clay. Use the bar graph to answer the questions.

1. Which sample has the most clay?

   _____

2. Which sample has the least clay?

   _____

3. What percent of sample C is made of clay?

   _____

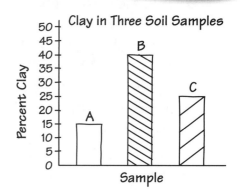

Clay in Three Soil Samples

F THE VENUS FLYTRAP

Pairwork

Some people grow Venus flytraps as houseplants. With a partner, use the library or
internet to learn how to care for a Venus flytrap. How long should the Venus flytrap
be in the sun each day? Should you feed it?

_____

_____

G WRITING Comparing and Contrasting

A friend wants to plant a garden. Your friend
asks what you know about different kinds of soil.
How are different kinds of soil alike? How are
they different? Write a paragraph comparing and
contrasting kinds of soil.

_____

_____

_____

_____

LAB Group Work Plant Leaves

Question What do plants need to live?

Procedure

1. Cut three pieces of aluminum foil or black paper. Each piece should be about twice as big as one of the plant's leaves.

2. Fold each piece of paper or foil in half. Slip the folded pieces over three of the plant's leaves. Use tape to close, covering the leaves.

3. Place the plant in a sunny window. Water it every two to three days.

   Safety Note: Wash your hands after handling the plant's leaves.

4. Predict what will happen to the leaves that are covered.

   _____

   _____

Materials
- potted plant
- aluminum foil or black paper
- tape

5. After ten days, carefully take the paper or foil off of the plant's leaves. What do you observe?

   _____

   _____

   _____

Analysis

1. What **effect** did covering the leaves produce? What **caused** this change?

   _____

   _____

2. Think about what you know about the function of a plant's leaves. **Infer** one thing that leaves need to do their job.

   _____

   _____

A VOCABULARY WORDS

Circle the word or words that complete each sentence.

Example: Roots / (Leaves) grow on stems.

1. Ferns are vascular / nonvascular plants.

2. Conifers produce flowering plants / cones.

3. Flowering plants / Mosses are a kind of vascular plant.

4. Ferns have roots / seeds and leaves.

5. Xylem / Phloem carries water from roots to leaves.

B VOCABULARY IN CONTEXT

Choose words from the box to complete the paragraphs.

mosses	nonvascular	phloem	roots
~~seedless~~	stems	vascular	xylem

Example: Mosses and liverworts are _____*seedless*_____ plants.

Different kinds of plants have different parts. (1) _____

plants, such as ferns and conifers, have roots. They also have

(2) _____ with tubes inside that help them distribute

food. (3) _____ moves water and minerals from the

plant's roots to its leaves. (4) _____ moves food from the

leaves to the other parts of the plant.

Other kinds of plants, such as mosses and liverworts, are

(5) _____ plants. This means that they do not have

(6) _____ or tubes. Nonvascular plants, such as

(7) _____ do not produce seeds.

📖 Student book pages 40–41

C FLOWERING PLANTS

Reading Strategy *Asking Questions*

Read **Flowering Plants** on page 40 of your student book. Write questions and answers about the reading to check your understanding.

> **Asking Questions**
> ✓ When you read, ask yourself questions to check your understanding.
> ✓ Use words like <u>what</u>, <u>where</u>, <u>when</u>, <u>why</u>, and <u>how</u> to form questions.

Questions	Answers
What are the parts of a flower?	A flower contains stamens and one or more pistils.

D WHAT IS A FERN?

Reading Strategy *Comparing and Contrasting*

Read **What Is a Fern?** on page 41 of your student book. Then answer the questions below.

> **Comparing and Contrasting**
> ✓ Tell how things are the same (compare).
> ✓ Tell how things are different (contrast).

Question	Flowering Plants	Ferns	Mosses
1. Do they reproduce with seeds or spores?			
2. Do they have roots?			
3. Do they have xylem and phloem?			

4. Use information from the chart to write two sentences. First tell how ferns and mosses are the same. Then tell how ferns and mosses are different.

_____

_____

_____

E SCIENCE SKILL Reading Steps in a Sequence

Read the paragraph below. Then answer the questions.

Conifers reproduce in the following way: First, they produce male cones and female cones. Then the male cones produce pollen. Next the wind takes the pollen from the male cones to egg cells on the female cones. Then pollen fertilizes the egg cells. Finally, seeds develop from those cells.

> **Reading Steps in a Sequence**
> ✓ Sequence tells you the order in which things happen.
> ✓ Words like first, then, and next help explain the sequence of something.

1. What is the first step in reproduction in conifers? _____

_____

2. What happens after the male cones produce pollen? _____

_____

3. What happens last in the reproduction of conifers? _____

_____

F HOW A SEED WORKS

Pairwork

With a partner, research the Coco-de-Mer palm tree. Find out what is special about its seeds. Write three sentences about what you learned.

_____

_____

_____

G WRITING Comparing and Contrasting

Think about ferns, mosses, and flowering plants. What plant parts do they have? Do they make seeds or spores? Where do they make them? Write a paragraph that compares and contrasts them.

> **Comparing and Contrasting**
> ✓ Tell how things are the same (compare).
> ✓ Tell how things are different (contrast).

_____

_____

_____

LAB **Group Work** Water Movement in Plants

Question How does water move through a plant?

Procedure

1. Add water to the glass until it is about 2 cm deep. Then add 15 drops of red food coloring.
2. Do not cut the leaves off the celery stalk. Use the knife to cut a notch 5 cm from the bottom of the stalk. Then cut 1 cm off the bottom of the stalk.

   Safety Note: Even a plastic knife can be sharp. Use caution.

3. Quickly put the bottom of the stalk in the water. Record the time in the chart to the right.
4. **Observe** the stalk every 10 minutes. Look for any color change in the stalk. Record your observations.
5. After 40 minutes, take the stalk out of the water. Record the time.
6. **Measure** how far the water moved up the stalk. Write your measurement.

Materials
• tall, clear plastic glass
• celery stalk with leaves
• red food coloring
• clock or watch
• plastic knife
• metric ruler
• water

Time	Color Changes

_____

7. Look for color changes above and below the notch. Record what you **observe.**

_____

Analysis

1. **Infer** why the stalk above the notch did not turn red. _____

   _____

2. Is celery a vascular or nonvascular plant? Explain your **conclusion.**

   _____

   _____

A VOCABULARY WORDS

Match the items on the left with the correct definitions.

Example: 6. sunlight   _6_ light energy from the sun

1. chloroplast   ____ cells in leaves that let water and air enter and leave

2. guard cells   ____ how green plants make food from sunlight

3. xylem   ____ plant tubes that carry food to the rest of the plant

4. photosynthesis   ____ plant tubes that carry things from roots to leaves

5. phloem   ____ part of the plant cell involved in photosynthesis

B VOCABULARY IN CONTEXT

Choose words from the box to complete the paragraph.

stomata	leaves	photosynthesis	roots	xylem
chlorophyll	sunlight	chloroplasts	soil	phloem

Example: Green plants are green because they contain _____*chlorophyll*_____.

Green plants make their own food and release oxygen during

(1) _____. This takes place in the (2) _____ in the

cells of green leaves. The (3) _____ of green plants need three things

to make food. They need energy from (4) _____, water, and carbon

dioxide. The water enters from the (5) _____ through the

(6) _____. It is carried to the leaves by (7) _____

tubes. Carbon dioxide enters through openings in leaves called

(8) _____. Once food has been made, it moves to other plant parts

by (9) _____ tubes.

C **PHOTOSYNTHESIS**

Reading Strategy *Asking Questions*

Read **Photosynthesis** on page 44 in your student book. Write questions and answers about the reading to check your understanding.

> **Asking Questions**
> ✓ When you read, ask yourself questions to check your understanding.
> ✓ Use words like <u>what</u>, <u>where</u>, <u>when</u>, why, and <u>how</u> to form questions.

Questions	Answers
What organisms can make their own food?	plants

D **TRANSPORT IN A PLANT**

Reading Strategy *Visualizing*

> **Visualizing**
> ✓ Make a picture in your mind.

Read **Transport in a Plant** on page 44 in your student book. Visualize a picture in your mind.
Draw a picture of a tree below. Use an arrow to show the path water takes in the tree. Label the arrow "xylem." Draw another arrow to show the path that food takes. Label that arrow "phloem." Explain your drawing to a classmate.

E SCIENCE SKILL Interpreting a Diagram

Read the information and look at the diagram. Then answer the questions.

This diagram of photosynthesis explains how plants make food. It has three parts. The materials needed by the plant are on the left side. The products of photosynthesis are on the right side. The arrow points toward the things that are made. Photosynthesis needs energy to work. It also needs the chlorophyll in green leaves. The energy and chlorophyll are not changed. They help the reaction happen.

> ### Interpreting a Diagram
> ✓ Diagrams help explain concepts.
> ✓ Diagrams can use labels, arrows, and words.

$$\text{carbon dioxide} + \text{water} \xrightarrow[\text{chlorophyll}]{\text{sunlight}} \text{sugar} + \text{oxygen}$$

1. What does the plant use to make food? _____

2. What else does the plant need for photosynthesis to work? _____

_____

3. What are the products of photosynthesis? _____

F ANNUAL TREE RINGS

Pairwork

Read **Annual Tree Rings** on page 45 in your student book. Then look at the picture on the right. Discuss the questions with your partner.

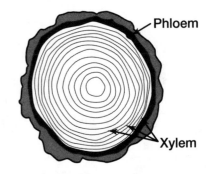

1. How old do you think the tree is?

2. For about how long (in years) did the tree have a lot of water? How can you tell?

G WRITING Applying Information

People benefit from green plants in many ways. Think about the products of photosynthesis. Tell about two ways. Write a paragraph.

> ### Applying Information
> ✓ Use information for a particular reason.

_____

_____

_____

_____

LIFE SCIENCE Photosynthesis • LAB

LAB **Group Work** The Oxygen Factory

Question How can you tell that plants might be producing oxygen?

Procedure

1. Pull several leaves off a cut end of a piece of elodea. Crush the cut end lightly.

   Safety Note: *Adult help needed. Your teacher must cut the plant. Keep the lamp away from water.*

2. Put the materials together as shown in the picture. Put the elodea in a funnel. Place the wide end of the funnel down in a wide-mouth container of water.

3. Add water and a pinch of baking soda to the test tube. Turn it over onto the end of the funnel. Make sure the opening of the test tube is under the water.

4. Put a lamp close to the container and turn it on. Be careful not to get the lamp wet.

5. What gas will form in the test tube? Write a prediction.

   _____

   _____

6. Count the number of bubbles that form in 10 minutes. Write that number in a data table. How many bubbles form in 1 minute? Write that number.

   _____

7. Turn off the light. Count the number of bubbles that form in 10 minutes. Write that number.

   _____

Materials
- elodea plant
- test tube
- wide-mouth container
- water
- lamp with 40-watt bulb
- baking soda
- clock
- single edge razor blade
- clear plastic funnel

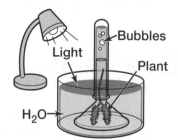

Analysis

1. What do you think the bubbles were? _____

   _____

2. Were more bubbles made when the light was turned on or when the light was turned off? How can you explain this? Write your **conclusion**.

   _____

   _____

A VOCABULARY WORDS

Write the vocabulary words in the correct side of the chart.

| air | ~~frog~~ | water | grosbeak | food | octopus | shark |
| turtle | crab | duck | raccoon | shelter | deer | |

What all animals need	Types of animals
	frog

B VOCABULARY IN CONTEXT

Choose words from the box to complete the paragraph.

| sharks | food | octopuses | frogs | raccoons |
| shelter | birds | water | ~~air~~ | deer |

Example: Land animals take in oxygen from the _____ air _____ they breathe.

All animals need the same things in order to live. Animals need

(1) _____ to keep their bodies from drying out and to keep cool.

Land animals like (2) _____, birds, or deer get water by drinking

or from food. Many animals use the oxygen in air, while some animals, such as

(3) _____ and octopuses, use oxygen from the water they live in.

Animals need energy in order to move about. They get energy from the

(4) _____ they eat. Large animals like (5) _____ eat

lots of grass. (6) _____ eat insects and small fish with their long

sticky tongues. Animals also need (7) _____, or a safe place to live.

Some animals like (8) _____ build nests high in tree branches.

(9) _____ find safe places to live in underwater caves or among

rocks.

📖 Student book pages 48–49

C KINDS OF ANIMALS

Reading Strategy *Using What You Know*

Think what you know about different kinds of animals. Write it in the chart. Then read **Kinds of Animals** on page 48 in your student book. Write what you learned in the chart.

> **Using What You Know**
> ✓ Think what you already know about the topic.
> ✓ Use what you already know to help you understand new information.

What You Know
All animals need air, water, food, and shelter.
What You Learned

D WHAT IS AN ANIMAL?

Reading Strategy *Facts and Examples*

Read **What Is an Animal?** on page 48 in your student book. Find facts about animals and write them in the chart. Think of examples of the facts.

> **Facts and Examples**
> ✓ Write down facts as you read.
> ✓ Write down an example for each fact.

Fact	Example
Animals eat food for energy.	An owl eats mice for food.

E SCIENCE SKILL Reading a Pie Chart

Mary asked 100 pet owners what kind of animal they owned. Use the pie chart she made to answer the questions.

Reading a Pie Chart

✓ A pie chart shows the parts of something. The size of the slice shows the amount.

1. What is the most common pet?

   _____

2. What percentage of pets are fish?

   _____

3. Are cats or birds more popular as pets?

   _____

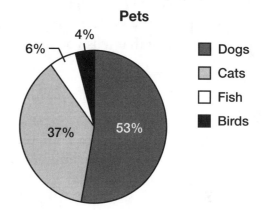

Pets

- Dogs
- Cats
- Fish
- Birds

4%

6%

37%

53%

F THE AMAZING OCTOPUS

Pairwork

Read the paragraph below. Then answer the questions.

The octopus is a soft-bodied sea animal. It has a large brain and keen eyesight. It has eight arms. It uses the suckers on its arms to catch shellfish that it uses for food. It moves by forcing a jet of water out of the funnel under its head. It can hide by squirting out a cloud of black ink. The female produces thousands of eggs, which hatch into young. Octopuses live in caves or hide among rocks on the sea floor.

How is the octopus the same as all other animals? How is it different? Make a list with your partner.

G WRITING Making Inferences

How do the suckers on the arms of octopuses help them? Write a paragraph.

Making Inferences

✓ Use what you know to make a decision.

_____

_____

_____

_____

47

LAB **Group Work** Animals

Question What animals live nearby?

Procedure

1. Go for a walk in a park, woods, or other outdoor place in your area. Walk quietly. What do you see or hear that tells you animals live nearby?

Materials
- pen or pencil

_____

_____

2. Look for animals. Look under pieces of wood or rocks. Look up in trees. Write the names of any animals that you observe in the chart. Then write down your observations. What are the animals doing? Where do they live?

Animal	Observations

Analysis

1. **Infer.** You know that animals need air, water, food, and shelter. How do you think the animals that you observed meet these needs?

_____

_____

_____

2. With your group, decide on a way to communicate what you observed to others in your class. Make a poster, write a short report, or talk to your class about the animals you saw on your walk.

A VOCABULARY WORDS

Circle the word or words that complete each sentence.

Example: A clam and a scallop both have a _____.

backbone (shell) sponge

1. A tapeworm or _____ can live inside other animals.

   heartworm   earthworm   lobster

2. Sponges, jellyfish, and _____ all live in the sea.

   centipedes   beetles   sea stars

3. Some invertebrates such as _____ have a hard outer case and spin webs.

   scallops   spiders   earthworms

4. The most common animals, called _____, do not have backbones.

   vertebrates   mammals   invertebrates

5. The _____ is a sea animal with a nearly clear, bell-shaped body.

   clam   jellyfish   sea star

B VOCABULARY IN CONTEXT

Choose words from the box to complete the paragraph.

| spider | backbones | shells | jellyfish | earthworm |
| invertebrates | tapeworm | scallops | lobsters | |

Example: Some invertebrates have _____shells_____.

Animals without (1) _____ are called (2) _____.

Some invertebrates like (3) _____ have soft bodies. Others have

shells like (4) _____. Still others have hard outer cases. Invertebrates

can live everywhere. We could see a(n) (5) _____ or a centipede in a

building. We can find a(n) (6) _____ in the soil. We can get a(n)

(7) _____ inside our own bodies. But many invertebrates, such as

(8) _____, sea stars, clams, and scallops, live in the sea.

📖 Student book pages 52–53

C ARACHNIDS

Reading Strategy *Using What You Know*

Think what you know about spiders. Write it in the chart. Then read **Arachnids** on page 52 in your student book. Write what you learned in the chart.

What You Know
Spiders build webs.
What You Learned

D METAMORPHOSIS

Reading Strategy *Scanning for Information*

Read questions 1–3 below. Then read **Metamorphosis** on page 52 in your student book. Write your answers.

Questions	Answers
1. What is metamorphosis?	
2. What hatches from a butterfly's eggs?	
3. What is the chrysalis?	

E SCIENCE SKILL Reading a Cycle Diagram

Read the passage below. Look at the cycle diagram. Then answer the questions.

Like a butterfly, a grasshopper's body changes. It goes through three stages of growth. It starts as an egg. Then it becomes a nymph. The young nymph grasshopper looks like the adult but has no wings. Finally, it develops wings, and grows into an adult grasshopper.

1. What are the three life stages?

   _____

2. What does the egg become after it hatches?

   _____

3. How is an adult grasshopper different from the young nymph grasshopper?

   _____

   _____

> **Reading a Cycle Diagram**
> ✓ In a cycle, things happen the same way over and over.

Life Cycle of a Grasshopper

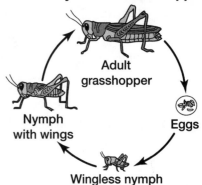

Adult grasshopper

Eggs

Wingless nymph

Nymph with wings

F HOW SPONGES WORK

Pairwork

Read **How Sponges Work** on page 53 in your student book. How is the sponge the same as all the other animals? How is it different? Make a list with your partner.

G WRITING Making Observations

Find a detailed picture of an insect in a book or on the internet. Does it have legs? Count its legs if it does. Try to see how many body parts it has. Does it have any other parts that you can see? What color is it? Write a paragraph.

> **Making Observations**
> ✓ Look at something closely to learn about it.

_____

_____

_____

_____

LAB **Group Work** Compare Invertebrates

Question How do invertebrates protect themselves?

Procedure

1. With your group, use a shovel to turn over a shovelful of soil. Separate the soil with the trowel. Observe the soil for living things.

   Safety Note: Wear gloves. Do not touch any of the invertebrates.

2. Make a list of all the invertebrates you can see in the soil. Make a chart similar to the one shown below in a notebook. Write a short description of each one.

Materials
- magazines with pictures of invertebrates
- shovel
- gloves
- garden trowel

Invertebrate name	Description or drawing	Hard body covering? Write *yes* or *no*.

3. Look through nature magazines or on the internet. When you see pictures of invertebrates, add them to your list.

4. Classify the invertebrates in your list into two groups. One group has shells or hard coverings. The other group of invertebrates is those without a shell or hard covering.

Analysis

1. **Compare** the two groups. Which group is better protected?

   _____

   _____

2. What are some other ways you could sort the invertebrates on your list?

   _____

   _____

A VOCABULARY WORDS

Complete the crossword puzzle
with the words in the box.

kangaroo	penguin
mammals	salamander
seahorse	humans

Across

1. you and your classmates
6. one kind of amphibian

Down

2. dogs and cats are in this
   group
3. one kind of fish
4. a mammal with a pouch
5. a bird that cannot fly

B VOCABULARY IN CONTEXT

Choose words from the box to complete the paragraph.

amphibians	~~backbones~~	vertebrates	bird	fish	frogs
mammal	flamingos	reptile	trout	penguin	

Example: Animals that have _____backbones_____ are called vertebrates.

There are five groups of (1) _____. Some live only in water, such

as the (2) _____ group. Two animals in this group are

(3) _____ and seahorses. Other groups, such as mammals and

reptiles, live on land. A bear is a kind of (4) _____ and a crocodile is

a(n) (5) _____. Animals that can live in the water or on land are

(6) _____. (7) _____ and salamanders are

amphibians. All the animals in the (8) _____ group live on land but

some can fly. (9) _____ are birds with long legs and pink feathers. A

bird that swims is the (10) _____.

C WARM-BLOODED AND COLD-BLOODED VERTEBRATES

Reading Strategy *Visualizing*

Read **Warm-blooded and Cold-blooded Vertebrates** on page 56 in your student book. Draw a picture of a warm-blooded vertebrate in your notebook. Show it in cold weather. Then draw a picture of a cold-blooded vertebrate in your notebook. Show it in cold weather. Explain your drawings to a classmate.

> **Visualizing**
> ✓ Make a picture in your mind.

D KANGAROOS ARE MAMMALS WITH POUCHES

Reading Strategy *Using Idea Maps*

Read **Kangaroos Are Mammals with Pouches** on page 57 in your student book. Then fill in the idea map with facts from the reading.

> **Using Idea Maps**
> ✓ Use idea maps to show the relationships between ideas.

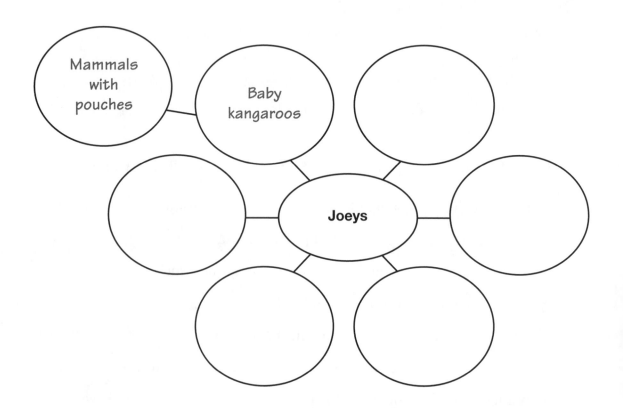

Mammals with pouches

Baby kangaroos

Joeys

E SCIENCE SKILL Comparing and Contrasting

There are three major groups of fishes. Look at the chart and answer the questions.

Jawless fishes	Cartilaginous fishes	Bony fishes
They have a backbone.	They have a backbone.	They have a backbone.
Their backbones are not made of bone.	Their backbones are not made of bone.	Their backbones are made of bone.
They do not have a jaw.	They have a jaw.	They have a jaw.
Sea lampreys are jawless fishes.	Sharks are cartilaginous fishes.	Trout are bony fishes.

How are the fish the same?

1. Sharks and trout: _____

2. Sea lampreys and sharks: _____

How are they different?

3. Trout and sharks: _____

4. Sharks and sea lampreys: _____

F KANGAROOS ARE MAMMALS WITH POUCHES

Pairwork

The koala is another type of animal with a pouch. Work with a partner. Use the internet or the school library to research this animal. List three facts about newborn koalas.

G WRITING Analyzing Information

Think about the difference between a newborn human and a newborn kangaroo. Which one crawls first? Why does it crawl? Which one crawls later? How does it go from place to place before it can crawl? Write a paragraph with your ideas.

_____

_____

_____

LAB Group Work Feathers

Question Do feathers keep a bird warm?

Procedure

1. With your group, fill one baggie full of feathers. Fill another baggie full of ice cubes. Leave one bag empty.
2. Place the empty baggie on the palm of your hand. Have another student place the bag of ice on top of the empty baggie. As soon as you feel the cold, say, "stop." Use the stopwatch to measure how long it takes you to feel the cold.
3. Repeat, using the baggie full of feathers instead of the empty baggie. Record your times in the chart.

Materials
- feathers
- zip-lock baggies
- ice cubes
- stopwatch

Name of student	With feathers	Without feathers

4. Everyone in your group should take a turn.

Analysis

1. What can you **conclude** about how birds stay warm in cold weather?

_____

2. What do you do to keep warm in cold weather? How does this **compare** to how birds stay warm?

_____

_____

3. How could you change the experiment to show what happens when oil gets on a bird's feathers?

_____

_____

📖 Student book pages 58–59

A VOCABULARY WORDS

Circle the word or words that complete each sentence.

Example: Bones / (Kidneys) are organs that remove wastes.

1. The lungs / brains are an organ found inside the chest.

2. A part of the body that looks like tubes is the kidneys / blood vessels.

3. Muscles / Skin is the largest organ in the human body.

4. The intestines / bones support the body and help it move.

5. The system of the body that digests food includes the stomach / lungs.

B VOCABULARY IN CONTEXT

Choose words from the box to complete the paragraph.

heart	muscles	lungs	blood vessels
skin	bones	brain	

Example: _____Skin_____ covers and protects your body.

Your body is made of many parts that often work together. The

(1) _____ controls all life activities such as breathing and

movement. The (2) _____ support the body. Along with

the brain and (3) _____, they help your body move. The

(4) _____ pumps blood to all body parts. The

(5) _____ take in air. Oxygen from the air is carried in blood

to all body parts. The blood moves through a system of small tubes

called (6) _____.

📖 Student book pages 60–61

C   ORGAN SYSTEMS

Reading Strategy *Facts and Examples*

Read **Organ Systems** on page 60 of your student book. Find facts about organ systems and write them in the chart. Think of examples of the facts.

> **Facts and Examples**
> ✓ Write down facts as you read.
> ✓ Write down an example for each fact.

Fact	Example
Your body has eleven organ systems.	They include the nervous system, digestive system, respiratory system, and excretory system.

D   THE CIRCULATORY SYSTEM

Reading Strategy *Sequencing*

Read **The Circulatory System** on page 61 of your student book. Then write the order in which blood moves around the body. Complete the cycle diagram.

> **Sequencing**
> ✓ Sequence tells the order in which things happen.
> ✓ Words like <u>before</u> and <u>after,</u> or <u>then</u> and <u>next,</u> can explain the sequence of something.

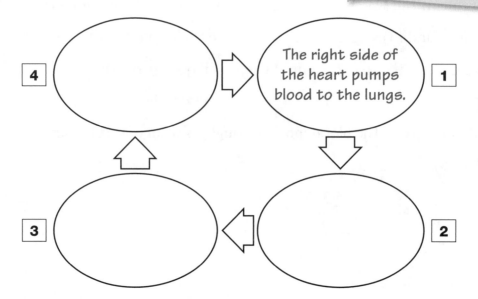

4

1 The right side of the heart pumps blood to the lungs.

3

2

E SCIENCE SKILL Concept Maps

Study the concept map on page 60 of your student book. Then look for the details that answer the questions.

Concept Maps
✓ Concept maps help organize information.
✓ The main idea is in the middle. Boxes show related details.

1. Which organ system helps you get rid of wastes?

   _____

2. Which organ system controls life activities such as breathing?

   _____

3. Which organ system helps you change food into a form your cells can use? What are its main organs? _____

   _____

4. What is the main job of the respiratory system? _____

   _____

F ORGAN SYSTEMS

Pairwork

Work with a partner. Use the internet or the school library to learn how the nervous system works. Then answer the questions.

1. What are the main parts of the nervous system? _____

   _____

2. What connects the brain with other parts of the body? _____

3. How do nerve cells communicate with the brain? _____

   _____

G WRITING Comparing and Contrasting

Compare the circulatory system to the nervous system. Write a paragraph.

Comparing and Contrasting
✓ Tell how things are the same (compare).
✓ Tell how things are different (contrast).

_____

_____

_____

_____

LAB **Group Work** Breathe In, Breathe Out

Question How do the lungs move gases in and out of the body?

Procedure

1. Make a model to discover how your lungs move air into and out of your body. Cut the plastic bottle in half. Save the top half of the bottle.
2. Pull a small round balloon through the neck of the bottle. Stretch the mouth of the balloon over the mouth of the bottle. Use a rubber band to hold the balloon in place. This balloon models one of your lungs.
3. Cut off the neck of the larger balloon. Stretch this balloon over the open end of the plastic bottle. Use another rubber band to hold the balloon in place as shown. This balloon models a muscle under your lungs.
4. Tape a small piece of cardboard to the bottom of the large balloon. This will make a handle you can use to make your model lung work.
5. Gently push and pull on the handle while holding the neck of the bottle. What do you observe?

Materials
- 1 medium size round balloon
- 1 small size round balloon
- tape
- plastic 1-liter bottle
- scissors
- 2 rubber bands
- piece of cardboard

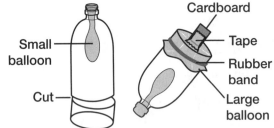

Small balloon
Cut
Cardboard
Tape
Rubber band
Large balloon

_____

6. Hold the bottle so the mouth is near your cheek. Move the handle in and out. Take turns so everyone in your group can try it. What do you feel?

_____

Analysis

1. What do you **observe** happening to the small balloon when you pull on the handle?

_____

2. There is a large muscle called the diaphragm under your lungs. What do you **infer** causes your lungs to fill with air and empty with every breath you take?

_____

_____

A VOCABULARY WORDS

Draw a line from each word to the phrase that tells about it.

1. chromosome

2. bulb

3. nucleus

4. vegetative
   reproduction

5. daughter cells

a. a form of sexual reproduction

b. each has the same chromosomes as the
   parent cell

c. plant part that can form a new plant

d. provides instructions to make new cells

e. contains chromosomes

B VOCABULARY IN CONTEXT

Choose words from the box to complete the paragraph.

asexual reproduction	parent cell	~~leaf~~	chromosomes
cell division/mitosis	nucleus	root	bulb
vegetative reproduction	daughter cells	stem	

Example: Tiny new plants can grow along one _____leaf_____ of a

kalanchoe plant.

Living things can make new cells by (1) _____. A cell has

chromosomes in its (2) _____. (3) _____ have the

plans for new cells. The (4) _____ makes copies of its chromosomes.

Then it divides into two (5) _____. Each new cell is like the parent

cell. (6) _____ happens when living things make new cells by

mitosis. Sometimes a whole new plant can be made by mitosis. This is called

(7) _____. Certain plant parts such as (8) _____,

(9) _____, (10) _____, or leaves can make new plants

by vegetative reproduction.

LIFE SCIENCE · Asexual Reproduction · **CONCEPTS**

C BACTERIA REPRODUCTION

Reading Strategy *Main Idea and Details*

Read **Bacteria Reproduction** on page 64 of your student book. Then complete the chart with details that support the main idea.

> **Main Idea and Details**
> ✓ The main idea of a paragraph is the big idea.
> ✓ Details support the main idea.

Main Idea:
Bacteria reproduce by asexual reproduction.

Detail	Detail	Detail

D MITOSIS

Reading Strategy *Scanning for Information*

Read questions 1–3 below. Then read **Mitosis** on page 64 of your student book. Write your answers.

> **Scanning for Information**
> ✓ Understand what information you need before reading.
> ✓ Read to find the information.

1. What are the four stages of mitosis?	
2. Where do chromosomes move in the second stage?	
3. What does the wall of the nucleus do in the last stage?	

E **SCIENCE SKILL** Looking for Patterns

Read the paragraph. Look at the chart. Then answer the questions.

Scientists use yeast cells to study how cells divide. Yeast is a kind of fungus. It is used to make bread. A yeast cell divides about every 90 minutes. Before it divides, it spends time growing or becoming larger. Look at the table below. It shows the rate of yeast cell reproduction.

Minutes	Number of Yeast Cells
0 (start)	1
90	2
180	4
270	8
360	16
450	

1. How many cells are there at 360 minutes?

   _____

2. What must each yeast cell do before it divides?

   _____

3. Predict how many cells there will be at the end of 450 minutes.

   _____

F **VEGETATIVE REPRODUCTION**

Pairwork

You notice that you have some new plants growing in your garden. You didn't plant them. They look the same as the plants in your neighbor's garden. His garden is just on the other side of the fence. Read **Vegetative Reproduction** on page 65 of your student book. Then work with a partner. Think of reasons why the plants in your garden are the same as your neighbor's plants.

   _____

   _____

G **WRITING** Analyzing Information

How do all the cells in runners, leaves, and berries of a strawberry plant become just like the cells in the parent plant? Write a paragraph.

   _____

   _____

   _____

   _____

LIFE SCIENCE Asexual Reproduction • LAB

LAB **Group Work** Model Mitosis

Question What are the steps of mitosis?

Procedure

1. **Make a model** of cell division. Put two pieces of construction paper together. Fold them in half to make a 4-page booklet.
2. Write the name of one stage of mitosis on each page of your booklet. Use the picture to make sure your model is assembled correctly. On the top page of your booklet, draw the outline of a large cell. Draw a circle to represent a nucleus.
3. Tie two pieces of yarn together in the middle. This models a double-stranded chromosome. Make eight double-stranded chromosomes from the yarn pieces.
4. Glue four double-stranded chromosomes in the nucleus of the prophase stage cell. Use the diagrams on page 64 as a guide. Label the model *nucleus* and *chromosomes*.
5. On the next piece of paper, draw the outline of one cell. Use the diagram on page 64 in your student book as a guide. Glue four double-stranded chromosomes inside the cell. Label this phase.
6. On the third piece of paper, draw the outline of one cell. Use eight single pieces of yarn as chromosomes. Label this phase.
7. On the bottom piece of paper, draw the outline of two cells. Use page 64 as a guide to draw the fourth stage. Label the *daughter cells.* Label this phase.

Materials
- 32 pieces of colored yarn, each 10 cm (about 4 in.) long
- 2 pieces of light colored construction paper
- scissors
- glue
- markers

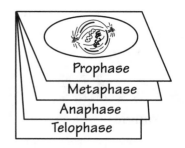

Analysis

1. What are the steps in cell division or mitosis? _____

   _____

2. What two important things happen during mitosis? Write your **conclusion.**

   _____

   _____

A VOCABULARY WORDS

Match the items on the left with the correct definitions.

Example: 7. cell division __7__ when a cell divides in two

1. sexual reproduction   _____ process in which sex cells are formed

2. parent cell   _____ egg cells or sperm cells

3. meiosis   _____ reproduction without sex cells

4. chromosomes   _____ reproduction by two parents

5. sex cells   _____ a cell that divides to form daughter cells

6. asexual reproduction   _____ structures that give instructions to
                                make new cells

B VOCABULARY IN CONTEXT

Choose words from the box to complete the paragraph.

sex cells	sexual reproduction	cell division
meiosis	chromosome(s)	~~parent cell~~

Example: In sexual reproduction a ____*parent cell*____ goes

through cell division two times.

   (1) _____ is a process in which two parents have

offspring. First, a parent cell goes through (2) _____

twice. This process is called (3) _____. It forms

(4) _____ with half the (5) _____

of the parent cell. One sex cell from each parent join to create the

offspring.

📖 Student book pages 68–69

C MEIOSIS AND SEX CELLS

Reading Strategy *Comparing and Contrasting*

Read the paragraph. Use it to complete the diagram.

   A parent cell has pairs of matching chromosomes. During cell division, small sections of these chromosomes can switch places with each other. This is called crossing over. This can make the chromosomes in the daughter cells different from the parent cell. The parent cell divides two times in meiosis to form a set of four cells. The daughter cells from meiosis have half as many chromosomes as the parent cell. These cells are called sex cells. Sex cells can be eggs or sperm. Sex cells from two parents join to make offspring.

> **Comparing and Contrasting**
> ✓ Tell how things are the same (compare).
> ✓ Tell how things are different (contrast).

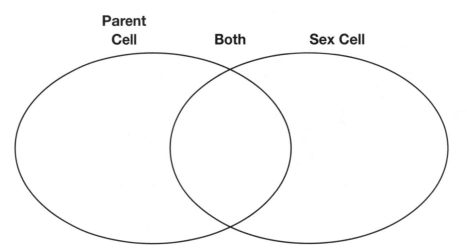

Parent Cell   Both   Sex Cell

D VARIATIONS

Reading Strategy *Cause and Effect*

Read **Variations** on page 69 of your student book. Then answer the questions.

> **Cause and Effect**
> ✓ The cause is what happens.
> ✓ The effect is the result of the cause.

1. *Cause* What can happen to chromosomes during meiosis?

   _____

2. *Effect* What is the result when this happens?

   _____

E SCIENCE SKILL Reading a Flow Chart

Some cells reproduce by meiosis. It is a process
with two cell divisions. Look at the flow chart on
page 68 of your student book. The flow chart shows
the steps in meiosis. Use it to answer the questions.

> **Reading a Flow Chart**
>
> A flow chart shows
> steps in a process.
> The arrows show the
> movement from one step
> to the next.

1. What does the process begin with?

   _____

2. What happens at the start of Meiosis II? _____

   _____

3. Where does the flow chart break in two? What happens here?

   _____

4. How many male sex cells become sperm cells? How many female sex cells
   become egg cells?

   _____

F VARIATIONS

Pairwork

Look at the photo of the puppies on page 69 in your student book. Work with a
partner. How are the markings and colors on the puppies' heads different? Write
two sentences.

_____

_____

_____

G WRITING Making Inferences

Why does sexual reproduction produce more
variation than asexual reproduction? Write a
paragraph.

> **Making Inferences**
>
> ✓ Use what you know to
> make a decision.

_____

_____

_____

_____

LAB **Group Work** Copying Chromosomes

Question Why must chromosomes divide in half during meiosis?

Procedure

1. Make a three-column table. Label the first column "Parent A." Label the second column "Parent B." Label the third column "Offspring." Place the beans in a pile.

Materials
- dried beans or other counters
- paper
- pencil

2. One person as "Parent A" takes a bean from the pile. Another person as "Parent B" takes another bean. The beans are "chromosomes" from each of two parents. Join them together.

3. Count the "chromosomes" in this first trial. Record the number that came from each "parent." Then record the total number of "chromosomes" in the third column. What do the joined beans stand for?

_____

4. Count out the same number of beans there were in the "offspring" in Step 3. This is the number of "chromosomes" from one "parent." Record the number. Count out the same number for the other "parent." Join the "chromosomes." Record the total number.

5. Repeat Step 4 three times. How many "chromosomes" are there in the "offspring"?

_____

Analysis

1. **Look for patterns** in your data. What happens each time you repeat Step 4?

_____

_____

2. Why must chromosomes divide in half during meiosis? Write a **conclusion**.

_____

_____

Gateway to Science Workbook • Copyright © Heinle, Cengage Learning

📖 Student book pages 70–71

Ⓐ VOCABULARY WORDS

Circle the word or words that complete each sentence.

Example: Genes are found on (chromosomes) / DNA.

1. Parents pass on traits / guanine to their children.

2. DNA is in the shape of a chromosome / double helix.

3. Eye color is passed from parents to children in their genes / traits.

4. Chromosomes are made of DNA / thymine.

5. Hair color is a base / trait.

6. Cytosine / Gene is a base.

7. DNA is made of four bases / genes.

8. DNA contains instructions / traits to build each part of your body.

9. Chromosomes are in the nucleus of cells / genes.

10. In science, a base is one kind of chemical compound / chemical recipe.

Ⓑ VOCABULARY IN CONTEXT

Choose words from the box to complete the paragraph.

double helix	adenine	~~traits~~	cytosine	thymine
guanine	genes	chromosomes	DNA	

Example: Parents pass on _____traits_____ to their children.

Parents pass traits to their children in their (1) _____.

Genes are found on (2) _____, which are made from

(3) _____. It is in the shape of a (4) _____,

which looks like a twisted ladder. The rungs of the ladder are made of

(5) _____, (6) _____,

(7) _____, and (8) _____.

📖 Student book pages 72–73

C **DOMINANT AND RECESSIVE TRAITS**

Reading Strategy *Comparing and Contrasting*

Read **Dominant and Recessive Traits** on page 72 in your student book. Then complete the chart about tongue rolling.

> **Comparing and Contrasting**
> ✓ Tell how things are the same (compare).
> ✓ Tell how things are different (contrast).

Tongue Rolling		
Offspring inherit two dominant genes.	**Offspring inherit one dominant gene and one recessive gene.**	**Offspring inherit two recessive genes.**
	Offspring can roll their tongues.	

D **PUNNETT SQUARES**

Reading Strategy *Summarizing*

Read **Punnett Squares** on page 73 in your student book. Write a summary below.

> **Summarizing**
> ✓ Write something in a shorter form.

_____

_____

_____

_____

_____

_____

_____

_____

E SCIENCE SKILL Reading a Punnett Square

In guinea pigs, black fur (B) is a dominant trait. White fur (b) is a recessive trait. The Punnett square below shows the possible offspring of two guinea pigs. Use the Punnett square to answer the questions.

Reading a Punnett Square

A Punnett square organizes information about traits. It shows how genes from two parents produce a trait.

	B	b
b	Bb	bb
b	Bb	bb

Guinea pig

1. Are the parents black or white? How do you know? _____

_____

2. Can the parents have white offspring? How do you know?

_____

_____

3. Can the parent with bb genes have black offspring? Explain.

_____

_____

F DOMINANT AND RECESSIVE TRAITS

Pairwork

With a partner, make a list of 5 traits you think are carried by genes. Trade your list with your partner. Compare your lists and talk about any differences.

G WRITING Applying Information

Brown eyes are dominant in people. Can the offspring of two parents with brown eyes have blue eyes? Why or why not? Write a paragraph.

Applying Information
✓ Use information for a particular reason.

_____

_____

_____

LAB Group Work Inherited Traits

Question What inherited traits are more common?

Procedure

1a. **Observe** each member of your group for the traits shown in the chart below. Then organize data from your observations in chart 1b.

Trait			Dominant	Recessive
Tongue rolling			can roll edges	cannot roll edges
Shape of hairline			pointed in the middle	not pointed
Freckles			freckles	no freckles
Earlobes			free	attached
Eyelash length			long	short

1b.

Trait	Shows dominant trait	Shows recessive trait
Tongue rolling		
Shape of hairline		
Freckles		
Earlobes		
Eyelash length		

2. Study your table. Compare your results with those of other groups in your class.

Analysis

1. Which traits are more common, dominant traits or recessive traits? Why do you think so? Write your **conclusion.**

_____

_____

_____

Gateway to Science Workbook • Copyright © Heinle, Cengage Learning

Ⓐ VOCABULARY WORDS

Circle the word or words that complete each sentence.

Example: A pouched (beak) / fossil is an adaptation that helps the pelican survive.

1. A change in an organism that helps it survive is a(n) subspecies / adaptation.

2. Living things that cannot reproduce with one another belong to different

   kingdoms / species.

3. Differences within the same species are called common ancestors / variations.

4. Organisms of the same species that can reproduce together, but have different

   variations, belong to different subspecies / kingdoms.

5. Remains of living things in rocks called variations / fossils show how they

   changed.

6. Two living things are closely related if they share a(n) common ancestor /

   adaptation.

Ⓑ VOCABULARY IN CONTEXT

Choose words from the box to complete the paragraph.

~~beaks~~	variations	organisms
subspecies	adaptations	species

Example: Over time, bird _____beaks_____ changed.

Arctic (1) _____ have (2) _____ that help them

survive in cold, snowy climates. The (3) _____ named snowshoe

hares, or *Lepus americanus,* are a group of animals that look like large rabbits.

All snowshoe hares have large feet. They help the hares walk on snow. Their fur

becomes white in winter to look like snow. This protects the hares from animals

that eat them. There are six different (4) _____ of the snowshoe

hare. Each has slightly different (5) _____. For example, the Virginia

snowshoe hare has brown fur in the summertime, the same color as the forest

where it lives.

📖 Student book pages 76–77

C THE THEORY OF EVOLUTION

Reading Strategy *Sequencing*

Read **The Theory of Evolution** on page 76 in your student book. Then put the steps below in order from 1–7 according to the theory of evolution.

_____ Some birds lived in different places and found different foods.

_____ Over time, the bird's beaks changed to help them eat new foods.

_____ Eventually, new species of birds that ate the new foods appeared.

_____ First, there were no birds on Earth, but there were dinosaurs.

_____ Later, some dinosaurs evolved into birds.

_____ Birds with beak variations that helped them find food survived.

_____ Birds that could not find food died out.

> **Sequencing**
> ✓ Sequence tells you the order in which things happen.
> ✓ Words like <u>before</u> and <u>later,</u> or <u>first</u> and <u>last,</u> can explain the sequence of something.

D NATURAL SELECTION

Reading Strategy *Cause and Effect*

Read **Natural Selection** on page 77 in your student book. Then write the missing cause and effect of variation in moths in the chart below. Remember: An effect of one cause can be the cause of a different effect.

> **Cause and Effect**
> ✓ The cause tells what happened.
> ✓ The effect is the result of the cause.

Cause	➡ Effect
Dark moths were easy to see on tree trunks.	Birds ate the dark moths.
Coal dust darkened trees.	Dark moths were hard to see.
	Birds stopped eating the dark moths.
Birds stopped eating the dark moths.	

Gateway to Science Workbook • Copyright © Heinle, Cengage Learning

E **SCIENCE SKILL** **Reading a Tree Diagram**

Study the tree diagram of birds on page 76 of your
student book. Then answer the questions.

> **Reading a Tree Diagram**
> ✓ The base shows the
>   common ancestor.
> ✓ The branches show
>   species descended from
>   the common ancestor.

1. What three kinds of birds are closely related to

   hummingbirds and swifts? _____

   _____

2. What bird is a common ancestor of gulls and cranes? _____

3. What birds are closely related to pelicans? _____

   _____

F **NATURAL SELECTION**

Pairwork

Work with a partner. Read the list of adaptations of leopards. Leopards are a kind of
wild cat that makes its home in forests or rocky places. They sleep during the day
and hunt at night. Talk about how these adaptations might help the leopard survive.
Write your ideas.

1. strong muscles _____

2. sharp claws _____

3. excellent eyesight; eye shape that controls amount of light _____

   _____

4. spotted coat _____

5. sharp hearing; ears that move _____

G **WRITING** **Recognizing Evidence**

How can you explain the theory of how living things
change over time? What evidence supports this
idea? Write a paragraph.

> **Recognizing Evidence**
> ✓ Recognize the facts that
>   support a theory.

_____

_____

_____

_____

LAB **Group Work** Model Natural Selection

Question How do variations help animals survive?

Procedure

1. Scatter the colored objects on the green sheet of construction paper. The paper is the "feeding area." The objects are the "insects."
2. Members of the group take on the role of birds looking for insects to eat. Each "bird" has a "nest" to collect the insects found in each 30-second flight over the paper.
3. One at a time, take turns going to the feeding area. Look for insects. Each bird takes 5 turns at the feeding area. The rules: Pick up only 1 insect each flight. Pick up only the insects you spot. It does not matter which color. Grab the first insect you see. Move quickly.
4. Each person takes 5 turns. Count how many insects of each color were collected. Complete the chart. Record how many "insects" of each color were collected.

Materials
- 2 large sheets of colored construction paper (1 green and 1 white)
- clock or watch
- 100 objects (pipe cleaners or yarn), 25 each in 4 colors (including green and black)

	Green Insects	Black Insects	_____ Insects	_____ Insects
Trial 1				
Trial 2				

5. Which color of food was hardest to find in Trial 1? _____

6. Repeat Steps 1–4 with the white sheet of construction paper. Record how many insects were collected in the second trial. Which color food was easiest to find this time?

_____

Analysis

1. How did blending in with the background affect how many insects were collected?

_____

2. Pollution makes the "feeding area" darker. Which "insects" do you think will survive best?

_____

📖 Student book pages 78–79

A VOCABULARY WORDS

Fill in the chart below with the names of two members of each kingdom. Then write a sentence about each kingdom.

Kingdom	Members of Kingdom	Sentence
animal kingdom	dog and worm	Fish are also members of the animal kingdom.
eubacteria kingdom	1.	2.
protist kingdom	3.	4.
fungi kingdom	5.	6.
plant kingdom	7.	8.
archeobacteria kingdom	9.	10.

B VOCABULARY IN CONTEXT

Choose words from the box to complete the paragraph.

animal	archeobacteria	bacteria	ferns
fungi	halophiles	methanogens	~~mold~~
mushrooms	pine trees	protist	six

Example: _____Mold_____ belongs to the fungi kingdom.

Living things can be placed into (1) _____ kingdoms. People

are part of the (2) _____ kingdom. (3) _____

and (4) _____ belong to the plant kingdom. Some people

eat (5) _____, which belong to the (6) _____

kingdom. (7) _____ belong to either the eubacteria kingdom or the

(8) _____ kingdom. (9) _____ and

(10) _____ are two types of archeobacteria. Seaweed belongs

to the (11) _____ kingdom.

C LEVELS OF CLASSIFICATION

Reading Strategy *Comparing and Contrasting*

Read the paragraph below. Then answer the questions.

> Comparing and Contrasting
> ✓ Tell how things are the same (compare).
> ✓ Tell how things are different (contrast).

All animals belong to the animal kingdom. Animals in the animal kingdom are divided into smaller and smaller groups. As the groups get smaller, the animals in each group become more alike. Bears are in the animal kingdom. Bears are sorted into smaller and smaller groups. All bears belong to the family Ursidae. Black bears, brown bears, and polar bears belong to the genus *Ursus*. Sun bears and giant pandas each belong to a different genus.

1. How are polar bears and sun bears the same? _____

   _____

2. How are black bears and polar bears alike? _____

   _____

3. How are sun bears and giant pandas different? _____

   _____

4. How are brown bears and sun bears different? _____

   _____

D USING DNA TO CLASSIFY

Reading Strategy *Restating*

Read **Using DNA to Classify** on page 80 in your student book. Use the Glossary in your student book to find the words you don't understand. Then use your own words to tell what the paragraph says.

> Restating
> ✓ Retell the meaning of a passage in your own words.

_____

_____

_____

_____

E SCIENCE SKILL Reading a Diagram

Look at the diagram on page 80 in your student
book. Then answer the questions.

1. Which animal does not belong to the Chordate
phylum?

_____

2. Which groups do both cheetahs and tigers belong to? _____

_____

3. Which animals do not belong to the same order as dogs? _____

_____

F TWO-PART NAMES

Pairwork

Read **Two-part Names** on page 81 in your student book. With a partner, use the
internet to find the two-part names of the animals listed below.

1. killer whale   _____

2. red kangaroo   _____

3. peregrine falcon _____

4. ocean sunfish   _____

5. electric eel   _____

G WRITING Interpreting Information

Classification systems put things that are similar
into groups. How does a food store group foods?
Why do they group them that way? Write a
paragraph.

_____

_____

_____

_____

LAB **Group Work** Classifying Organisms

Question How are different living things classified?

Procedure

1. With your group, look through magazines. Cut out pictures of living things.

   Safety Note: *Be careful when you use the scissors.*

2. Go through the pictures you cut out. What kingdom does each one belong to? Sort the pictures into piles according to kingdom.

3. Use the pictures you classified to make a poster. Glue the groups of pictures onto the poster board. Label each group.

Materials
- scissors
- old magazines with pictures of different living things
- poster board
- glue

Analysis

1. Which kingdom did the greatest number of pictures belong to? Which kingdom did the least number of pictures belong to?

   _____

2. **Compare** the living things you **classified.** How are organisms in each kingdom similar? How are they different?

   _____

   _____

   _____

   _____

A VOCABULARY WORDS

Circle the one word in each group that doesn't belong. Tell why the word does not belong with the other words in the group.

Example: biome / (house) / rain forest _____A rain forest is one kind of biome._____

_____A house is neither a biome nor a rain forest._____

1. tundra / taiga / species _____

_____

2. grassland / community / population _____

_____

3. deciduous forest / rain forest / tundra _____

_____

B VOCABULARY IN CONTEXT

Choose words from the box to complete the paragraphs.

grassland	community	deciduous forest	desert
~~biomes~~	rain forest	ecosystem	tundra
species	population	taiga	

Example: Around the world, different kinds of plants and animals live in large

areas called _____biomes_____.

Buffalo live in dry (1) _____ biomes. Cactuses live in hot

(2) _____ biomes. The cold (3) _____ biome has

polar bears but no trees. The (4) _____ biome has many evergreen

trees. Many insects live in steamy, wet (5) _____ biomes. Maple trees

and deer live in (6) _____ biomes. The living and nonliving parts of

a biome make up a(n) (7) _____.

A group of the same (8) _____ of animal might live in the same

area. They make up a(n) (9) _____. All the different populations in

an area make up a(n) (10) _____.

C **ECOLOGICAL SUCCESSION**

Reading Strategy *Main Idea and Details*

Read **Ecological Succession** on page 84 of your student book. Fill in the chart with the main idea and details that support the main idea.

> **Main Idea and Details**
>
> ✓ The main idea of a paragraph is the big idea.
> ✓ Details support the main idea.

Main Idea		
Detail Most change in nature is slow.	**Detail**	**Detail**

D **DESERT BIOMES**

Reading Strategy *Key Sentences*

Read **Desert Biomes** on page 84 of your student book. Then complete the chart with key sentences about desert biomes.

> **Key Sentences**
>
> ✓ Key sentences tell important facts about a topic.

Desert temperatures are from 20°C to 30°C.

+

1.

+

2.

=

Desert Biomes

E SCIENCE SKILL Reading a Time Line

The time line below shows how a forest grew
again after a fire. Use the time line to answer the
questions.

Reading a Time Line

✓ A time line shows what
happens at points over
time.

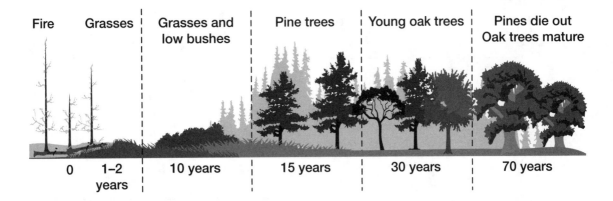

| Fire | Grasses | Grasses and low bushes | Pine trees | Young oak trees | Pines die out Oak trees mature |

| 0 | 1–2 years | 10 years | 15 years | 30 years | 70 years |

1. What plants were left after the fire? _____

2. What kind of trees are there 15 years after the fire? _____

3. How long did it take for the oak trees to completely replace the pine trees?

_____

F THE KANGAROO RAT'S ECOSYSTEM

Pairwork

Work with a partner. Use the internet to learn more about kangaroo rats and
where they live. How do they survive in hot, dry conditions? Why are they called
kangaroo rats?

G WRITING Analyzing Evidence

There is an empty lot with grass growing in it near
your school. Predict what will probably happen
to plants in the lot over the next ten years. What
evidence is your prediction based on? Write a paragraph.

Analyzing Evidence

✓ Study all the facts.

_____

_____

_____

_____

Name ______________________ Date ______________________

Student book pages 82–85

LAB Group Work Studying a Biome

Question What living and nonliving things do you find in a biome?

Materials
- magazines
- poster board
- reference books/the internet
- markers
- glue

Procedure

1. Choose a biome to study. Write its name.

   ____

2. Read about the plants, animals, temperatures, and amount of rain the biome receives each year.
3. Use the chart below to write information about your biome.

Biome name	Kinds of plants	Kinds of animals	Average temperature	Average rainfall

4. On a piece of poster board, draw or use pictures from magazines to show the living and nonliving things in your biome.

Analysis

1. Is your biome hot or cold? Is it wet or dry? ______________________

   ____

2. Choose one animal. Tell why your biome is a good place for this animal to live in.

   ____

   ____

A VOCABULARY WORDS

Circle the word or words that complete each sentence.

Example: Frogs are the (consumers) / producers in a food chain.

1. Producers get their energy from eating plants / sunlight.

2. Green plants use sunlight to make decomposers / food.

3. Plants are food for carnivores / herbivores.

4. Consumers / Decomposers break down wastes.

5. Bobcats and some owls are carnivores / decomposers.

6. Many food chains in one area form a producer / food web.

B VOCABULARY IN CONTEXT

Choose words from the box to complete the paragraph.

consumers	producers	herbivore	food
food chain	carnivore	food web	

Example: A _____food web_____ is made of many food chains.

Plants and animals need energy in order to live. They get energy from

(1) _____. Plants are (2) _____. They change sunlight

into energy they can use for growth. Plants also store energy. Animals are

(3) _____. A(n) (4) _____ gets energy by eating plant

parts. The plant's stored energy moves to the animal that eats it. A(n)

(5) _____ is an animal that eats other animals. It gets the energy

stored in the animals' bodies. A(n) (6) _____ shows how energy

moves through plants and animals in one geographic area.

C **AN ENERGY PYRAMID**

Reading Strategy *Asking Questions*

Read **An Energy Pyramid** on page 88 in your student book. Then write questions and answers about the reading to check your understanding.

> **Asking Questions**
> ✓ When you read, ask yourself questions to check your understanding.
> ✓ Use words like <u>what</u>, <u>where</u>, <u>why</u>, and <u>how</u> to form questions.

Questions	Answers
What does an energy pyramid show?	An energy pyramid shows how much energy moves up to the next level.

D **SYMBIOSIS**

Reading Strategy *Facts and Examples*

Read **Symbiosis** on page 88 of your student book. Find facts about symbiosis and write them in the chart. Think of examples of the facts.

> **Facts and Examples**
> ✓ Write down facts as you read.
> ✓ Write down an example for each fact.

Facts	Examples
Symbiosis occurs when two different kinds of organisms have a close relationship.	Honeybees and flowers have a close symbiotic relationship.

E SCIENCE SKILL Interpreting an Illustration

Read the paragraph and look at the picture. Answer the questions.

An energy pyramid is an illustration. It explains how energy moves through an area. Many plants and animals live in watery areas. This picture shows how energy moves in an underwater environment.

An Energy Pyramid

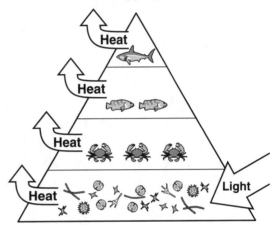

1. How does an underwater environment get energy?

   _____

   _____

2. Where are the producers in the energy pyramid?

   _____

   _____

3. What do the arrows in the illustration show?

   _____

F PREDATORS AND THEIR PREY

Pairwork

Work with a partner. Make a list of prey animals that other animals hunt. Then list ways each animal can hide or escape from predators.

G WRITING Applying Information

Think about a pet such as a dog or a fish. How does its relationship with its owner show mutualism? Write a paragraph.

_____

_____

_____

LAB **Group Work** Model an Energy Pyramid

Question How can you make a model of an energy pyramid?

Procedure

1. Look at pictures of different environments. Choose one to model. You might pick a desert, forest, tundra, grassland, or smaller area to study. Talk about the organisms that live there. Each member of the group should choose several living things from that area.

2. Write the name of one of the organisms or draw its picture on a card. Tape one end of a piece of string to the card. Continue until you have cards for all of the living things.

3. Tape the cards onto the poster paper. Put the producers near the bottom. Put the consumers above them. Tape the loose end of each string to the card of the organism that receives energy from the first organism.

4. Remove some cards from the paper. Observe what happens to the ends of the strings. Record your observations.

   _____

5. With your group, draw a picture of the energy pyramid for your environment.

Materials
- magazines or picture books showing different environments
- 30 index cards
- 30 long pieces of string
- large sheet of poster paper
- tape and markers

Analysis

1. How does your model show how energy moves through an area?

   _____

   _____

2. What happened when you removed some cards? Where did the energy go?

   _____

   _____

3. **Predict** what would happen if one of the living things were to disappear from the energy pyramid.

   _____

   _____

A VOCABULARY WORDS

Label the diagram with words from the box.

| condensation | evaporation | ~~ocean water~~ | precipitation | runoff |

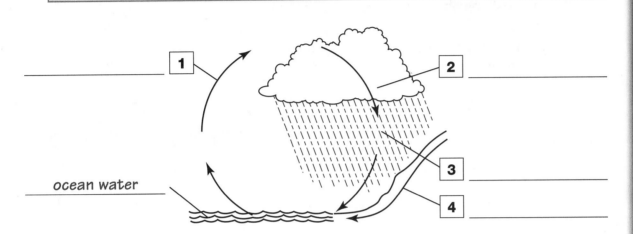

ocean water

B VOCABULARY IN CONTEXT

Choose words from the box to complete the paragraph.

| condensation | cloud | evaporation | groundwater | cycle |
| runoff | snow | ~~water~~ | water vapor | |

Example: One kind of cycle in nature is the _____water_____ cycle.

   A(n) (1) _____ occurs again and again. (2) _____

begins when the sun heats Earth's water. The water changes into

(3) _____ that rises into the air. When water vapor cools,

(4) _____ happens. Tiny droplets of water join together to form

a(n) (5) _____. The droplets become big and heavy. They fall to

Earth as rain or (6) _____. Some of the water that falls goes into

the ground. It becomes (7) _____. The rest of the water goes into

streams, rivers, and lakes as (8) _____.

C THE NITROGEN CYCLE

Reading Strategy *Using a KWL Chart*

Fill in the first two columns of the chart before you read. Write sentences about what you already *know* about nitrogen and bacteria in the first column. Write questions about what you *want* to know in the second column. Then read **The Nitrogen Cycle** on page 92 in your book. Fill in the L column of the chart with information that you *learned*.

> **Using a KWL Chart**
> ✓ Identify what you already know, what you want to know, and what you learned about a topic.

	K what I already *know*	W what I *want* to know	L what I *learned*
nitrogen			
bacteria			

D THE OXYGEN-CARBON DIOXIDE CYCLE

Reading Strategy *Scanning for Information*

Read questions 1–3 below. Then read **The Oxygen-Carbon Dioxide Cycle** on page 92 in your student book and find the answers.

> **Scanning for Information**
> ✓ Understand the information you need before reading.
> ✓ Read to find the information.

1. What gas do plants need?	
2. What gas do animals need?	
3. Which living things give off carbon dioxide?	

Gateway to Science Workbook • Copyright © Heinle, Cengage Learning

E SCIENCE SKILL Reading a Model

Look at the model of the nitrogen cycle on page 92 in your student book. Then answer the questions.

1. Where do bacteria in the soil get nitrogen? _____

   _____

2. What other living things use the changed nitrogen? _____

   _____

3. What do soil bacteria release into the air when they break down wastes?

   _____

F PLANTS IN THE WATER CYCLE

Pairwork

Work with a partner. Read **Plants in the Water Cycle** on page 93 in your student book. Look at a picture of a plant or at a real plant. Then discuss and write answers to the questions below.

1. What plant part takes in water? _____

2. Where does transpiration occur in the plant? _____

3. How does the water move from the roots? _____

   _____

4. How does the water vapor get into the air from the plant? _____

   _____

G WRITING Thinking About Systems

Think about cycles of nature. How do humans and houseplants depend on each other for things they need? Write a paragraph.

_____

_____

_____

_____

LAB **Group Work** Water Cycle

Question What causes the water cycle?

Procedure

1. Use a graduated cylinder to measure 150 mL of water. Pour the water into a plastic cup.

   Safety Note: Wipe up any spills right away.

2. Place the plastic cup of water into a zip-top plastic bag. Seal the bag tightly. Do not let any of the water spill out of the cup.

3. Place the bag with the cup in it in a sunny window. Make sure none of the water spills out of the cup.

4. Leave the cup in the window for several days. What do you observe?

   _____

   _____

5. After a week, carefully open the plastic bag. Take out the cup.

6. Measure the amount of water in the cup. Then measure the amount of water in the bottom of the bag. Add the two numbers together.

   _____

> **Materials**
> • plastic cup
> • zip-top plastic bag
> • graduated cylinder
> • water

Analysis

1. How did the amount of water you started with **compare** to the total amount in step 6?

   _____

2. What parts of the water cycle did you observe? What step can you **infer** took place?

   _____

3. What **caused** the water to evaporate? _____

   _____

Gateway to Science Workbook • Copyright © Heinle, Cengage Learning

A VOCABULARY WORDS

Draw a line from each word to the phrase that tells about it.

1. hibernation

2. stimulus

3. migration

4. response

5. phototropism

6. estivation

a. the movement of animals during a particular season

b. a growth response of green plants to light

c. period of inactivity in animals due to hot/dry conditions

d. spending winter in a deep sleep-like state

e. a loud noise is an example of this outside cause

f. protecting your ears from a loud noise is an example

B VOCABULARY IN CONTEXT

Choose words from the box to complete the paragraph.

migration	stimuli	~~response~~
estivation	hibernation	phototropism

Example: A change in living things as a result of stimuli is

called a _____response_____.

A change in seasons brings many changes to the environment. These are called

(1) _____. Animals respond to seasonal changes in different ways.

Some animals move to a different place. This is called (2) _____.

Other animals like bears sleep during the winter. This deep sleep to survive in

winter without food is called (3) _____. Still other animals like

snails and mud turtles sleep during dry, hot summer days. This is called

(4) _____. Animals are not the only things that respond to changes

in their surroundings. Some plants grow toward light. Others grow away from light.

The plant's response to light is called (5) _____.

C PLANT RESPONSES

Reading Strategy *Making Inferences*

Read the paragraph. Then answer the question below.

> **Making Inferences**
> ✓ Use what you know to make a decision.

Living things react to stimuli in two ways. They can either move toward them or away. Plants respond to gravity. This is called gravitropism. They can respond to gravity in both ways. The root grows downward. It grows toward gravity. The stem grows upward. It grows away from gravity.

Carrots, beets, and radishes come from plant roots. Where is the source of the stimulus that helps these vegetables grow? Explain why you think so.

_____

_____

_____

D WATCHING PLANTS MOVE

Reading Strategy *Main Idea and Details*

Read **Watching Plants Move** on page 96 in your student book. Then complete the chart with details that support the main idea.

> **Main Idea and Details**
> ✓ The main idea of a paragraph is the big idea.
> ✓ Details support the main idea.

Main Idea: Plants make other types of movements.		
Detail Flower buds open slowly.	**Detail**	**Detail**

E SCIENCE SKILL Interpreting Time-Lapse Photos

Some photographs show how things change. Look at the time-lapse photographs of a plant shoot growing in response to light. Answer the questions below.

1. Which photograph shows the younger plant? How do you know?

   _____

   _____

2. In what direction was the light coming in the second photo? How do you know?

   _____

   _____

F BEHAVING BY INSTINCT

Pairwork

Work with a partner. Choose an animal. You might choose a bear, whale, bee, bird, or some other animal that you want to learn about. Find out about its behavior. Use library books or the internet. Talk about the behaviors with your partner. Are they reflexes, instincts, or learned behavior? List what you decide in the chart.

Animal	Reflex	Learned Behavior	Instinct

G WRITING Integrating Information

Choose an animal. Think about its behaviors. Think how reflexes help the animal. What actions are learned behaviors? How are they learned? Think about its instincts. Write a paragraph.

_____

_____

_____

_____

LAB Group Work Features of an Environment

Question What happens to animals when the environment changes?

Procedure

1. Look at pictures of animals. Try to find pictures of the same animals in different seasons. Talk about what each animal needs to live.
2. Talk about each animal's environment. Is it cold or warm? Are there plants and trees? Are there other animals?
3. Talk about how each animal's environment can change. Then fill in the table.

> **Materials**
> • magazines or books showing photos of animals in the wild

Type of Animal	What does the animal need?	How does the animal's environment change?

Analysis

1. How do features of an animal's environment change? _____

_____

_____

2. What effect do these changes have on the animals? _____

_____

_____

Name _____ Date _____

📖 Student book pages 98–99

A VOCABULARY WORDS

Read each statement. Decide if it is true or false. If it is true, circle **T**. If it is false, circle **F** and change the sentence to make it true.

Example: The seed fern is an endangered species. T or (F)

      The seed fern is an extinct species. _____

1. An endangered species no longer has any living members. T or F

_____

2. The whooping crane is an extinct bird that could not fly. T or F

_____

3. A hedgehog cactus is an extinct species that lives in the desert. T or F

_____

4. The quagga is an extinct animal that looked like a zebra. T or F

_____

B VOCABULARY IN CONTEXT

Choose words from the box to complete the paragraphs.

black rhino	dinosaurs	~~dodo~~	endangered species
extinct species	mammoth	seed fern	

Example: The _____dodo_____, a bird that could not fly, became extinct

      in 1694 AD.

Some types of animals that once lived on Earth no longer exist. They are

(1) _____. Large reptiles called (2) _____ are extinct.

The (3) _____, which looked like an elephant, is also extinct. Some

plants are extinct, too, such as the (4) _____.

    (5) _____ are in danger of becoming extinct. One example is the

(6) _____, a rhinoceros that lives in Africa.

C TIGERS IN DANGER

Reading Strategy *Evaluating*

Read **Tigers in Danger** on page 100 in your student book. Then answer the question.

What can we do to save the tigers from becoming extinct?

_____

_____

_____

_____

> **Evaluating**
> ✓ Form opinions, make judgments, and develop ideas from reading.

D SAVING RAIN FOREST PLANTS

Reading Strategy *Cause and Effect*

Read **Saving Rain Forest Plants** on page 100 in your student book. Read the causes in the left column. Write possible effects in the right column.

> **Cause and Effect**
> ✓ The cause tells what is happening.
> ✓ The effect is the result of the cause.

Cause ➡	Effect
Plants have been used for medicines for centuries.	Scientists study plants to find new medicines.
Many rain forest plants could become extinct.	1.
Scientists are trying to save the rain forests.	2.

E SCIENCE SKILL Reading a Map

Read the paragraph and study the map on page 100 in your student book. Then answer the questions.

> **Reading a Map**
> ✓ A map gives information about where something is happening.

Human activities can harm plants and animals. People may disturb the places where they live. Then it becomes difficult to find enough food or space to live. This is one reason plants and animals become endangered or extinct. Hunters and sickness are other reasons. Some species are in danger because they live only in a small area. Space on islands is limited. As a result, the number of island animals is small. Once their numbers drop below a certain number, the group may not recover. When there are fewer animals, anything that endangers them may wipe out the entire group.

1. Look at where tigers lived before. Which extinct tigers lived on islands?

   _____

2. Which two subspecies of tiger live in very small areas? Why are they

   endangered? _____

   _____

3. Which subspecies is in more danger—Indo-Chinese tigers or Sumatran tigers?

   Explain your answer. _____

   _____

F BALD EAGLES RECOVER

Pairwork

Read **Bald Eagles Recover** on page 101 in your student book. Talk about the reading with your partner. Make two lists. List the reasons many bald eagles died. List the reasons they are recovering.

G WRITING Making Inferences

Why is saving the rain forests important to people and the world? Write a paragraph.

> **Making Inferences**
> ✓ Use what you know to make a decision.

_____

_____

_____

_____

LIFE SCIENCE **Conservation • LAB**

LAB Group Work Water Pollution

Question What are some effects of water pollution?

Procedure

1. Yeast are tiny living things. When they eat sugar, they produce a gas called carbon dioxide.
2. With a marker, label 2 plastic cups A and B. Fill Cup A half way with warm water. Add 1 packet of yeast and 1 spoonful of sugar. Stir to mix.
3. Fill Cup B half way with warm water. Add 1 packet of yeast and 1 spoonful of sugar.
4. Pour a little cooking oil into the water in Cup B. Then add a few spoonfuls of vinegar. Oil spills are one form of pollution that affects living things in water. Stir.
5. Make a prediction about which cup will have a negative effect on the growth of the yeast. Write your prediction.

_____

6. After 10 minutes, observe both cups. What do you observe?

_____

Materials
- water
- plastic cups
- marker
- paper labels
- plastic spoons
- sugar
- yeast
- oil
- vinegar

Analysis

1. What evidence do you **observe** that yeast can produce carbon dioxide?

_____

2. How does the yeast's activity in Cup A **compare** to the yeast's activity in Cup B?

_____

_____

3. Which cup modeled polluted water? What can you **infer** about how water pollution affects living things?

_____

_____

_____

A VOCABULARY WORDS

Write sentences with the words in the chart.

solar system	Earth, Venus, and Mars are part of our solar system.
galaxy	1.
star	2.
space	3.
planets	4.
telescope	5.

B VOCABULARY IN CONTEXT

Choose words from the box to complete the paragraph.

planets	radio telescope	solar system
space	stars	~~telescope~~

Example: A _____telescope_____ lets you see things that are far away.

The sun, Earth, and seven other (1) _____ are part of our

(2) _____. (3) _____ is the area beyond Earth.

A galaxy is a huge system of (4) _____ dust, and gas in space.

To find out where a star is in a galaxy, scientists use a (5) _____.

101

📖 Student book pages 104–105

C DISTANCES IN SPACE

Reading Strategy *Scanning for Information*

Read questions 1–3 below. Then read **Distances in Space** on page 104 of your student book and find the answers.

1. How many kilometers is an astronomical unit (AU)?

   _____

2. How many kilometers is a light-year?

   _____

3. How many light-years from Earth is Proxima Centauri?

   _____

> **Scanning for Information**
> ✓ Understand the information you need before reading.
> ✓ Read to find the information.

D THE MILKY WAY GALAXY

Reading Strategy *Main Idea and Details*

Read **The Milky Way Galaxy** on page 104 of your student book. Use the information to complete the chart with details that support the main idea.

> **Main Idea and Details**
> ✓ The main idea of a paragraph is the big idea.
> ✓ Details support the main idea.

Main Idea: The Milky Way is a spiral galaxy.		
Detail	**Detail**	**Detail**

E **SCIENCE SKILL Reading Numbers in a Table**

The table below shows distances from Earth to some of the brightest stars in the sky. Look at the table and answer the questions.

Reading Numbers in a Table

✓ When you read a table with numbers, find the unit of measure. Make sure you understand the measuring system.

1. What units are the distances measured in?

_____

2. Which two stars are closest to Earth? What distances are they?

_____

_____

Star	Distance (in light-years)
Aldebaran	65
Betelgeuse	425
Deneb	2,600
Procyon	11.4
Rigel	775
Sirius	8.6
Vega	25

3. Which two stars are farthest from Earth? What distances are they?

_____

_____

4. How much farther from Earth is Betelgeuse than Aldebaran? _____

F **TELESCOPES**

Pairwork

Work with a partner. Find information about refracting and reflecting telescopes on the internet or in the school library. Answer the questions below.

1. How are they alike? _____

_____

2. How are they different? _____

_____

G **WRITING Applying Information**

Imagine you are on a spaceship traveling through the Milky Way. Write a letter to a friend. Describe what you see.

Applying Information

✓ Use information for a particular reason.

_____

_____

_____

_____

LAB **Group Work** Distances in Space

Question How can you model distances in space?

Materials
- craft beads
- meter stick or tape measure
- masking tape
- marker

Procedure

1. The table shows distances from the sun. Multiply each distance by 10 centimeters. In your model of the solar system, 1 AU equals 10 centimeters. This is called the *scale*.

Planet	Distance from Sun (in AU)	Scale Distance (in cm)	Bead Color
1. Mercury	0.39	3.9	
2. Venus	0.72		
3. Earth	1		
4. Mars	1.5	15	
5. Jupiter	5.2		
6. Saturn	9.5		
7. Uranus	19.2		
8. Neptune	30.1	301	

2. Choose a yellow bead to represent the sun. Choose eight other beads to represent the planets of the solar system. Record the colors in the table.
3. Stick a piece of tape on the floor and label it "sun." Place the yellow bead on it.
4. Measure the scale distances from the sun bead. For example, measure 3.9 centimeters away from the sun bead for Mercury. Use tape to mark the distance. Write "Mercury" on the tape and place your Mercury bead on the tape.
5. Repeat these steps for each planet.

Analysis

1. Proxima Centauri is about 268,000 AU from the sun. If you wanted to **model** this distance, how many centimeters would your scale distance be?

_____

2. It takes about 8 minutes for light from the sun to reach Earth. How much **time** would it take light from the sun to reach Mars?

_____

A VOCABULARY WORDS

Match the items on the left with the correct definitions.

Example: 6. white dwarf __6__ forms after a red giant shrinks

1. nebula   _____ a very large main sequence star

2. star   _____ a cloud of dust and gas

3. sun   _____ a medium-sized star

4. constellations _____ shapes made by groups of stars

5. supergiant   _____ a hot ball of glowing gases

B VOCABULARY IN CONTEXT

Choose words from the box to complete the paragraph.

supernovas	main sequence star	black holes
red giant	white dwarf	supergiants
neutron stars	sun	

Example: Our _____sun_____ is a medium-sized star.

A (1) _____ uses hydrogen as fuel. When it starts to

burn out, it swells and becomes a (2) _____. Then it

shrinks and becomes a (3) _____. Some very large

main sequence stars become (4) _____. This type of star

is much larger than our sun. Some of these stars explode and become

(5) _____. Some others become (6) _____,

which are about the size of a small city. Other supergiants become

(7) _____. Because of their very strong gravity, nothing can

escape from them.

C STAR MAGNITUDE

Reading Strategy *Main Idea and Details*

Read the paragraph. Use it to complete the chart.

Scientists group stars by brightness or magnitude. Some stars look brighter than others. So each star has a magnitude number. A very bright star has a low magnitude number. A dim star has a high magnitude number. Stars that are closer to Earth look brighter than stars that are far from Earth.

> **Main Idea and Details**
> ✓ The main idea of a paragraph is the big idea.
> ✓ Details support the main idea.

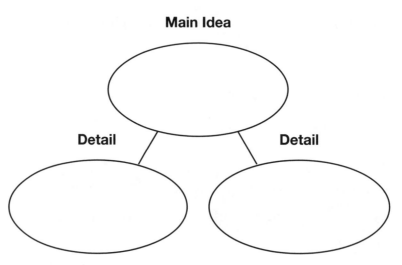

Main Idea

Detail　　　　**Detail**

D THE HERTZSPRUNG-RUSSELL DIAGRAM

Reading Strategy *Scanning for Information*

Read questions 1–3 below. Then read **The Hertzsprung-Russell Diagram** on page 108 of your student book and find the information.

> **Scanning for Information**
> ✓ Understand what information you need before reading.
> ✓ Read to find the information.

1. What does the Hertzsprung-Russell Diagram do?	
2. What different groups of stars are in the diagram?	
3. How does the diagram show temperature?	

E **SCIENCE SKILL** **Reading a Diagram**

The H-R diagram arranges stars in groups. The side shows how bright stars are. The temperature is shown on the bottom. Look at the H-R diagram on page 108 of your student book. Use the H-R diagram to answer the questions.

> **Reading a Diagram**
> ✓ A Hertzsprung-Russell Diagram (H-R diagram) arranges stars in groups. It shows brightness and temperature of stars.

1. Are supergiants bright or dim stars?

   _____

2. Where are the white dwarfs found on the diagram?

   _____

3. How do white dwarf stars compare with the sun?

   _____

   _____

F **PICTURES IN THE SKY: CONSTELLATIONS**

Pairwork

Work with a partner. Use the internet to find the names of two constellations. Read about each group of stars. Write two or three sentences telling what you learned about the two constellations.

_____

_____

_____

_____

G **WRITING** **Applying Information**

Explain the difference between the sun and a supergiant star. Include information on size, magnitude, and temperature. Write a paragraph.

> **Applying Information**
> ✓ Use information for a particular reason.

_____

_____

_____

_____

LAB Group Work Star Magnitude

Question How does distance affect brightness?

Procedure

1. Set two equally bright flashlights next to each other on a desk. Turn them on. Turn off the room lights.

   Materials
   • two equally bright flashlights

   Safety Note: If turning off the lights makes the room very dark, only dim the lights. Do not look directly into the light from the flashlights.

2. Look at the flashlights from the other side of the room. Observe the brightness of each flashlight. Talk about what you saw with your group. Write what you saw.

   _____

3. Move one of the flashlights to a desk closer to your group. What do you think will happen to the brightness of each flashlight? Write your prediction.

   _____

   _____

4. Again, look at the flashlights from the other side of the room. Talk about your observations with your group.

Analysis

1. How is what you saw like stars in the sky? _____

   _____

   _____

2. Will a star close to Earth or farther from Earth appear brighter? Write your **conclusion.**

   _____

   _____

Ⓐ VOCABULARY WORDS

Cross out the word that does not belong in each group. Tell why the word you crossed out does not belong.

Example: dwarf planet   Earth   ~~moon~~   Uranus   meteoroid

Why? A moon orbits a planet. The others do not. _____

1. Neptune   sun   Jupiter   Mercury   Saturn

   Why? _____

2. orbit   Venus   asteroid   Mars   comet

   Why? _____

Ⓑ VOCABULARY IN CONTEXT

Choose words from the box to complete the paragraphs.

asteroids	comets	dwarf planets	Earth	Jupiter
Mars	meteoroids	Mercury	moons	Neptune
orbit	~~sun~~	Uranus	Venus	

Example: All objects in our solar system orbit the _____sun_____.

Our solar system has eight planets and three (1) _____. Planets

(2) _____ the sun, and (3) _____ orbit planets. The

planet we live on, (4) _____, has only one moon. The planet

(5) _____ has about 60 moons. (6) _____ is the

planet closest to the sun, and (7) _____ is the farthest from the sun.

Earth is between (8) _____ and (9) _____. The planet

between Saturn and Neptune is (10) _____.

Our solar system also has (11) _____, which are balls of ice, rock,

and gases. (12) _____ are large chunks of rock and metal.

(13) _____ are smaller chunks of rock and metal.

📖 Student book pages 112–113

C JUPITER AND ITS MOONS

Reading Strategy *Visualizing*

Read the information about **Jupiter and Its Moons.** Visualize a picture in your mind. Draw the picture in your notebook. Explain the drawing to a classmate.

> **Visualizing**
> ✓ Make a picture in your mind.

> Jupiter is the fifth planet from the sun. It is the largest planet. It is made mostly of gases. The Great Red Spot is a large area on the surface of Jupiter. It is a giant storm three times larger than Earth.
>
> About 60 moons move around Jupiter. The 4 largest moons are Callisto, Europa, Ganymede, and Io.

D A FAMOUS COMET

Reading Strategy *Cause and Effect*

Read the first paragraph of **A Famous Comet** on page 112 in your student book. Use the information to complete the chart.

> **Cause and Effect**
> ✓ The cause tells what happened.
> ✓ The effect is the result of the cause.

Cause	➡	Effect
A comet's orbit can take it close to the sun.		
		A glowing object can sometimes be seen from Earth.

E SCIENCE SKILL Interpreting an Illustration

The illustration shows the order of the eight planets from closest to farthest from the sun. Write the name of each planet on the lines below.

1. _____   5. _____

2. _____   6. _____

3. _____   7. _____

4. _____   8. _____

F DWARF PLANETS

Pairwork

Before 2006, scientists thought Pluto was a planet. In 2006, they decided it was a dwarf planet. Why? Work with a partner. Use the internet to find more information.

_____

_____

_____

G WRITING Making a Prediction

A large comet is traveling through our solar system. It is moving closer to the sun. What do you think you will see in the sky? Write a paragraph.

Making a Prediction

✓ Tell what you think is going to happen.

_____

_____

_____

_____

EARTH SCIENCE • Our Solar System • LAB

LAB Group Work Scale Models

Question How do solar system objects compare in size?

Procedure

1. Make a scale model of Mercury. Look at the chart below to see how big to make the circle. Use the ruler to set the protractor at the right distance. Use the protractor to draw a circle. Label the circle *Mercury.* In this model, 6,368 km = 5 cm.

Solar System Object	Radius of Model
Mercury	1.9 cm
Venus	4.7 cm
Earth	5.0 cm
Mars	2.7 cm
Pluto	0.9 cm
Moon	1.4 cm
Ganymede	2.1 cm
Callisto	1.9 cm
Io	1.4 cm
Europa	1.2 cm

Materials
- meter stick
- 2 sheets of construction paper
- metric ruler
- protractor
- pencil
- scissors

2. Make models of the other solar system objects the same way. Label each model.
3. Cut out each circle. Put the circles on a table or desk. Sort the models into three groups: *Planets, Moons,* and *Dwarf Planets.* Which solar system models are in each group? List their names below.

Safety Note: Be careful when you use the scissors.

Planets: _____

Moons: _____

Dwarf Planets: _____

Analysis

1. Put the models in order from largest to smallest. **Compare** the sizes of Mercury, Pluto, Ganymede, and Callisto.

_____

_____

2. What can you **conclude** about the sizes of planets, moons, and dwarf planets?

_____

_____

📖 Student book pages 114–115

A VOCABULARY WORDS

Circle the word that completes each sentence.

Example: Earth orbits / (tilts) on its axis.

1. The sun / moon is a huge ball of fire in the sky.

2. The angle at which something slopes is called its rotation / tilt.

3. The year is divided into four parts called orbits / seasons.

4. An orbit / axis is an imaginary line through the middle of something.

5. Rotate means the same thing as tilt / spin.

6. Earth revolves / tilts around the sun.

7. If something moves through a complete circle, it seasons / rotates.

8. The sun / moon orbits Earth.

9. It takes Earth 24 hours to complete one orbit / rotation.

B VOCABULARY IN CONTEXT

Choose a word from the box to complete the paragraph.

axis	day	Earth	moon	night
rotate	~~seasons~~	spin	sun	

Example: The _____seasons_____ happen because Earth tilts on its axis.

The (1) _____ gives heat and light to (2) _____.

It takes 24 hours or one (3) _____ for Earth to completely

(4) _____ or (5) _____ once on its

(6) _____. At (7) _____ your part of Earth rotates

away from the sun. Then you can often see the (8) _____ in

the sky.

C **LENGTH OF DAY AND NIGHT**

Reading Strategy *Using What You Know*

Think what you know about day and night. Why does Earth have day and night? How long are days and nights? Write what you know in the chart. Then read **Length of Day and Night** on page 116 in your student book. Write what you learned in the chart.

> **Using What You Know**
> ✓ Think what you already know about the topic.
> ✓ Use what you already know to help you understand new information.

What You Know
One day and night is 24 hours long.
What You Learned

D **SUMMER AND WINTER SEASONS**

Reading Strategy *Drawing Conclusions*

Read **Summer and Winter Seasons** on page 116 in your student book. Then answer the questions. Look at a globe or a world map to help you.

> **Drawing Conclusions**
> ✓ Make a decision after you think about all the facts.

1. It is fall in Australia. What season is it in North America? _____

   _____

2. The northern half of Earth is tilting toward the sun. What season is it in Canada?

   _____

3. The southern half of Earth is tilting toward the sun. What season is it in Europe?

   _____

Gateway to Science Workbook • Copyright © Heinle, Cengage Learning

E SCIENCE SKILL Making Observations

Depending on where you are on Earth, summer may begin in June or in December. The chart below shows the month of each season in the United States and in Australia. Use the chart to answer the questions.

Making Observations

✓ By studying something closely, you can learn more about it.

Season	Months in United States	Months in Australia
Winter	December, January, February	June, July, August
Spring	March, April, May	September, October, November
Summer	June, July, August	December, January, February
Autumn	September, October, November	March, April, May

1. In which country is it warmer in December? _____

2. In which country is it more likely to snow in January? _____

3. In what season is October in Australia? _____

F PHASES OF THE MOON

Pairwork

Read **Phases of the Moon** on page 117 in your student book. Then work with a partner. Place objects on a desk to show the position of the sun, the moon, and Earth in situations (1) and (2) below. Explain the positions of the sun, the moon, and Earth to another pair.

1. Full moon phase. The moon looks like a big, full circle in the sky during this phase.

2. New moon phase. We can't see the moon during this phase.

G WRITING Making Inferences

Sometimes when you look at the moon in the night sky, you see only a small curve or crescent shape. Which phase do you think this moon is in? Write a paragraph.

Making Inferences

✓ Use what you know to make a decision.

_____

_____

_____

_____

LAB **Group Work** Make a Model of Earth's Movements

Question How does Earth move?

Procedure

1. Choose one person from your group to hold the basketball. This person should stand still.
2. Have another person hold the tennis ball. This person walks slowly around the first person in a large circle. This person should spin the tennis ball while walking.
3. A third person should hold the ping-pong ball near the tennis ball. This person moves around the person with the tennis ball in small circles, while spinning the ball.
4. Complete one full circle around the basketball.

Materials
- tennis ball
- ping-pong ball
- basketball

Analysis

1. What did this **model** show? What did the basketball stand for? What did the tennis ball model? What did the ping-pong ball model?

   _____

   _____

   _____

2. What part of the **model** stood for one year? What movement stood for one day?

   _____

   _____

3. Based on your model, **compare** the motions of the moon and Earth.

   _____

   _____

A VOCABULARY WORDS

Circle the word or words that best complete each sentence.

Example: The moon pulling on Earth's water causes eclipses / (tides.)

1. When something blocks sunlight, it produces a shadow / tide.

2. The ocean water rises during high tide / low tide.

3. The water level falls near the shore during high tide / low tide.

4. The moon passes between the sun and Earth in a solar eclipse / lunar eclipse.

5. A total eclipse / partial eclipse occurs when the moon is completely in shadow.

6. Earth passes between the sun and the moon in a solar eclipse / lunar eclipse.

7. Part of the sun is blocked by the moon in a total eclipse / partial eclipse.

B VOCABULARY IN CONTEXT

Choose words from the box to complete the paragraphs.

high tide	solar eclipse	lunar eclipse	low tide
shadows	~~moon~~	tides	eclipse

Example: The closest object to Earth is the _____moon_____.

Although it is small, the moon affects Earth in many ways. The moon

pulling the ocean water creates (1) _____. When the water

rises there is a(n) (2) _____. When the water falls there is a(n)

(3) _____.

When the moon and Earth block sunlight they create (4) _____.

When a space object casts a shadow on another body, it causes a(n)

(5) _____. There are different kinds of eclipses. When the moon

casts its shadow on Earth, it causes a(n) (6) _____. When the Earth

casts its shadow on the moon, it causes a(n) (7) _____.

📖 Student book pages 120–121

C HIGH AND LOW TIDES

Reading Strategy *Visualizing*

Read **High and Low Tides** on page 120 of your student book. Visualize a beach at high and low tide in your mind. Then draw one picture of a beach at low tide and another of the same beach at high tide. If you need more space, draw the pictures in your notebook.

> **Visualizing**
> ✓ Make a picture in your mind.

D TOTAL AND PARTIAL ECLIPSES

Reading Strategy *Cause and Effect*

Read **Total and Partial Eclipses** on page 120 of your student book. Look at the photos below the reading. Write the missing causes or effects to complete the chart.

> **Cause and Effect**
> ✓ The cause tells what happened.
> ✓ The effect is the result of the cause.

Cause	➡	Effect
All the sun's or moon's light is blocked.		*total eclipse*
Part of the moon passes through the darkest part of Earth's shadow.		1.
2.		partial eclipse of the sun
The moon blocks the sun completely.		3.
4.		total lunar eclipse; The moon is completely covered in shadow.

Name _____ Date _____

E SCIENCE SKILL Contrasting Photos

Look at the photos of tides on page 118 of your
student book. Then read the times listed in the
chart below and answer the questions.

1. What time was the top picture taken? Explain.

_____

_____

2. What time was the bottom picture taken?
Explain.

_____

_____

Contrasting Photos

✓ Tell how photos are
different.

Tides in France, March 29	
Time	**Height (m)**
2:57 a.m.	2.67
8:24 a.m.	5.53
3:26 p.m.	2.09
9:08 p.m.	5.75

F HOW THE SUN AFFECTS TIDES

Pairwork

Read **How the Sun Affects Tides** on page 121 of your student book. Look at the
drawings with your partner. List two facts about spring tides and two facts about
neap tides.

Spring Tides

1. _____

2. _____

Neap Tides

3. _____

4. _____

G WRITING Recognizing Cause and Effect

Your friend tells you she built a beautiful sand castle
on the beach. She left to eat lunch and when she
came back later that day, the castle was gone.
Explain what happened. Write a paragraph.

Recognizing Cause and Effect

✓ Tell what happened
(cause).

✓ Tell the result of the
cause (effect).

_____

_____

_____

_____

LAB **Group Work** Solar Eclipse

Question Does a solar eclipse make all of Earth dark?

Procedure

1. Use the marking pen to label a paper plate "Earth."
2. Tape the paper plate flat against a wall. Try to choose a wall that is far from any windows.
3. Stick the sharp end of a pencil into a styrofoam ball. Label the styrofoam ball "moon."
4. Turn off the lights. Shine the flashlight on the paper plate so that the light just covers the plate.
5. Hold the ball so that it is between the flashlight and the paper plate. The ball should make a dark shadow on the paper plate about 3–4 centimeters across.

Materials
- sharpened pencil
- paper plate
- tape
- flashlight
- small styrofoam ball (about the size of a ping-pong ball)
- marker
- centimeter ruler

Analysis

1. Draw the shadow(s) that you **observed** on the paper plate below or in your science notebook.

2. Does a solar eclipse make all of Earth dark? What can you **infer** about the shadow that the moon casts on Earth during an eclipse?

_____

_____

Ⓐ VOCABULARY WORDS

Circle the word or words that complete each sentence.

Example: (Astronauts) / Satellites receive special training for space travel.

1. A space probe / space suit is special protective clothing worn by astronauts.

2. Astronauts travel in space shuttles / space probes.

3. A rocket takes off from a spacecraft / launchpad.

4. Astronauts can live on booster rockets / space stations for months.

5. External fuel tanks / Booster rockets send spacecraft into orbit.

6. A space shuttle / space suit can travel into space and back several times.

7. A space probe / launchpad is similar to a satellite because both collect information.

8. Space shuttles and rockets are examples of astronauts / spacecraft.

Ⓑ VOCABULARY IN CONTEXT

Choose words from the box to complete the paragraphs.

astronauts	~~launchpad~~	satellites	spacecraft
space probes	space shuttles	space station	space suits

Example: Many spacecraft take off from the _____launchpad_____ in Cape Canaveral, Florida.

Some types of (1) _____ carry people, while others do not.

(2) _____ carry people called (3) _____,

who are trained to travel in space. They wear special clothing called

(4) _____. Astronauts can live and work in space for months

on the (5) _____.

Scientists send (6) _____ into orbit around Earth. They launch

(7) _____ to study other planets. They do not carry people. They are

just sent into space to collect information.

📖 Student book pages 124–125

C EARLY SPACE EXPLORATION

Reading Strategy *Scanning for Information*

Read the questions below. Then read **Early Space Exploration** on page 124 of your student book and find the answers.

1. What happened in 1926?

   _____

   _____

2. What happened in 1945?

   _____

   _____

3. What happened in 1957?

   _____

   _____

> **Scanning for Information**
> ✓ Understand the information you need before reading.
> ✓ Read to find the information.

D WALKING ON THE MOON

Reading Strategy *Making Inferences*

Read **Walking on the Moon** on page 124 of your student book. Why do you think Neil Armstrong and Buzz Aldrin collected rocks and took pictures on the moon?

_____

_____

> **Making Inferences**
> ✓ Use what you know to make a decision.

Name _____ Date _____

E SCIENCE SKILL Reading a Time Line

The time line below shows events in space exploration. Use the time line to answer the questions.

> **Reading a Time Line**
>
> ✓ A time line shows what happens at points over time.
>
> ✓ Read a time line from left to right.

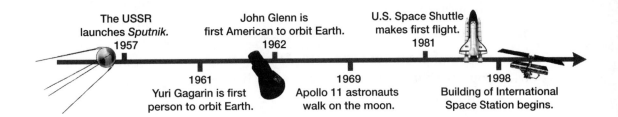

The USSR launches *Sputnik.* 1957

John Glenn is first American to orbit Earth. 1962

U.S. Space Shuttle makes first flight. 1981

1961 Yuri Gagarin is first person to orbit Earth.

1969 Apollo 11 astronauts walk on the moon.

1998 Building of International Space Station begins.

1. When did the U.S. Space Shuttle make its first flight? _____

2. When did building begin on the International Space Station? _____

3. John Glenn orbited Earth in 1962. How many years later did the Apollo 11 astronauts walk on the moon?

_____

F INTERNATIONAL SPACE STATION

Pairwork

Work with a partner. Think of astronauts on the International Space Station. Make a list of the ways life is different there.

G WRITING Integrating Information

Would you like to become an astronaut and work on the International Space Station? Why or why not? Write a paragraph.

> **Integrating Information**
>
> ✓ When you integrate information, you bring together parts to make a whole idea.

_____

_____

_____

_____

_____

LAB **Group Work** Life in Space

Question What is it like to live on the ISS?

Procedure

1. Look at pictures of homes in magazines and catalogs. Cut out pictures that show different rooms in a home.

    Safety Note: Be careful when you use the scissors.

2. Name each different kind of room. Talk about what you use that room for. Then make a list of all the things you do each day in your home.

    _____

    _____

3. Look at pictures of astronauts on the ISS. Make a list of the things astronauts do when they are on the ISS.

    _____

    _____

Materials
- home decorating magazines or catalogs
- photos of astronauts aboard the ISS
- scissors

Analysis

1. You cannot feel Earth's gravity on the ISS. You would be weightless and float around. Which of your daily activities would be difficult if you were weightless? Why?

    _____

    _____

    _____

2. **Compare** life on Earth to life on the ISS. What is the same? What is different?

    _____

    _____

    _____

EARTH SCIENCE   Space Exploration • LAB

Ⓐ VOCABULARY WORDS

For each group of words, circle the word that is **not** the same type of mineral or rock. Write why the mineral or rock is different.

Example: quartz /(granite)/ diamond

Granite is a rock. Quartz and diamond are minerals.

1. sandstone / granite / basalt

_____

2. limestone / sandstone / marble

_____

3. slate / basalt / marble

_____

Ⓑ VOCABULARY IN CONTEXT

Choose words from the box to complete the paragraph.

minerals	marble	~~quartz~~	sedimentary rock
metamorphic rock	diamond	crystals	sandstone
igneous rock	granite		

Example: The mineral _____quartz_____ is made of silicon and oxygen.

   (1) _____ are solids found naturally on Earth. Some minerals,

like quartz and (2) _____, are (3) _____. All rocks are

made of minerals. One kind of rock is formed when bits of sand, soil, and shells

are pressed together. It is called (4) _____. (5) _____

is a sedimentary rock. A second kind of rock is formed when melted rock cools. It

is called (6) _____. (7) _____ is an igneous rock. A

third kind of rock is formed when rocks get very hot and are pressed together deep

underground. It is called (8) _____. (9) _____ is a

metamorphic rock.

EARTH SCIENCE · Minerals and Rocks · CONCEPTS

C CLASSIFYING ROCKS

Reading Strategy *Main Idea and Details*

Read **Classifying Rocks** on page 128 of your student book. Then complete the chart with details that support the main idea.

> **Main Idea and Details**
> ✓ The main idea of a paragraph is the big idea.
> ✓ Details support the main idea.

Main Idea: Rocks are classified by how they form.		
Detail Igneous rocks form when melted rock cools.	**Detail**	**Detail**
Detail	**Detail**	**Detail**

D THE ROCK CYCLE

Reading Strategy *Sequencing*

Read **The Rock Cycle** on page 128 of your student book. Use numbers to order the sentences below.

> **Sequencing**
> ✓ Tell the order in which things happen.

___3___ Layers of sediment are pressed together.

_____ Weathering breaks down rock into sediment.

_____ Sedimentary rock is formed.

_____ Rivers carry the sediment away.

E **SCIENCE SKILL** Interpreting a Rock Cycle Diagram

Look at the diagram of the rock cycle on page 128 of your student book. Then answer the questions.

1. How does igneous rock change into metamorphic rock?

   _____

   _____

2. How do heat and pressure change sedimentary rock? _____

   _____

3. What changes metamorphic rock into sedimentary rock? _____

   _____

   _____

> **Interpreting a Rock Cycle Diagram**
>
> ✓ Any rock can change into any other kind of rock.
>
> ✓ Arrows show the processes that change rocks.

F **CLASSIFYING ROCKS**

Pairwork

Work with a partner. Make a drawing of a sedimentary rock. Then make a drawing of an igneous rock. Finally, make a drawing of a metamorphic rock. Label each kind of rock. Then, write a sentence under each picture that tells how the rock formed.

G **WRITING** Hypothesizing

Think about the processes that change rocks. How do you think water helps form sedimentary rock? Write a paragraph.

> **Hypothesizing**
>
> ✓ Tell what you think happens. Give reasons to support your ideas.

_____

_____

_____

_____

_____

LAB **Group Work** Metamorphic Rock

Question How does sedimentary rock become metamorphic rock?

Procedure
1. Pinch the clay into pieces. Use all colors. Some pieces should be big, and some should be small.
2. Layer the pieces of clay on top of each other to make a pile.
3. Use a soup can to flatten the pile. Press hard.
4. Use a plastic knife to cut your flattened "rock" open.

Materials
- modeling clay (several colors)
- plastic knife
- soup can

Analysis
1. Describe the pile of clay before you flattened it. What kind of rock did this **model?**

_____

_____

2. Describe the clay after you flattened it. What did the inside look like when you cut it open? What kind of rock did this **model?**

_____

_____

3. What part of the rock cycle did you **model** with the soup can?

_____

_____

A VOCABULARY WORDS

Label the drawing with words from the box.

inner core	lower mantle
crust	upper mantle
outer core	

1. _____

2. _____

3. _____

4. _____

5. _____

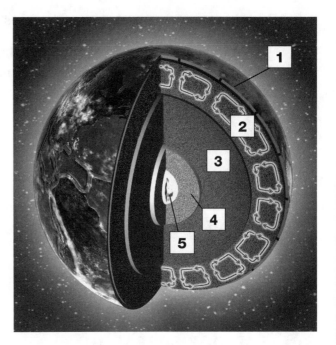

B VOCABULARY IN CONTEXT

Choose words from the box to complete the paragraph.

outer core	upper mantle	~~inner core~~
crust	lower mantle	continents

Example: The _____*inner core*_____ of Earth is made of solid metal.

Around Earth's inner core is the (1) _____. This layer is liquid

metal. Above the outer core is Earth's mantle. The (2) _____ is

hotter and softer than the (3) _____. The land on Earth's surface is

called the (4) _____. Above water, the crust forms our

(5) _____, and below water it is the floor of the oceans.

C CONTINENTAL DRIFT

Reading Strategy *Inferring from Evidence*

Read the paragraph and answer the questions.

> **Inferring from Evidence**
> ✓ Make a guess about something from facts you know.

Scientists found fossils of the same plants and animals from two different places: South America and Africa. Long ago, these two places were connected.

1. What can you infer about fossils from North America and Europe?

_____

2. A scientist found fossils of the same animals in Antarctica and Australia. What do the fossils suggest about these two places?

_____

D SEAFLOOR SPREADING

Reading Strategy *Sequencing*

Read **Seafloor Spreading** on page 132 of your student book. Then use numbers to order the sentences below.

> **Sequencing**
> ✓ Tell the order in which things happen.

___4___ Magma cools and forms rock on the ocean floor.

_____ A crack forms between the plates.

_____ New rock pushes the plates farther apart.

_____ Plates under the sea move apart.

_____ Magma from Earth's mantle rises into the crack.

Name _____   Date _____

E **SCIENCE SKILL Reading a Map**

Look at the map of Pangaea on page 132 of your
student book. Use it to answer the questions.

Reading a Map

✓ North, south, east, and
west tell where places are
on a map.

1. Which continent is north of Europe?

_____

2. Which continent is west of Europe?

_____

3. Which continents border Antarctica?

_____

F **PLATE TECTONICS**

Pairwork

Look at the map of Earth's plates on page 133 of your student book. Work with a
partner. Make a list of all the plates that have continents or land on them. Make a
list of the plates that are under oceans.

Plates with land:

_____

_____

Plates under oceans:

_____

_____

G **WRITING Applying Information**

How are seafloor spreading, continental drift, and
plate tectonics related? Write a paragraph.

Applying Information

✓ Use information for a
particular reason.

_____

_____

_____

_____

Gateway to Science Workbook • Copyright © Heinle, Cengage Learning

131

LAB Group Work Pangaea

Question How did the continents fit together long ago?

Procedure

1. Put a sheet of tracing paper on the world map. Center it over North America. Trace around the edges of North America. Label your tracing.
2. Repeat until you have traced each continent. Label each continent after you trace it.
3. Cut out each continent. Lay them out on a desk or a table.

   Safety Note: Be careful when you use the scissors.

4. Can you make Pangaea? See if you can fit your continents together. Slowly move them into their present positions.

Materials
- world map
- tracing paper
- scissors

Analysis

1. In your **model** of Pangaea, what continents were touching North America?

   _____

   _____

2. Use your model to **predict** where the continents will be in the future. Draw a picture.

Name _____ Date _____

📖 Student book pages 134–135

Ⓐ VOCABULARY WORDS

Write words from the box in the correct column of the chart.

canyon	lake
mesa	mountain
ocean	plain
river	

Types of land	Types of water
canyon	

Ⓑ VOCABULARY IN CONTEXT

Choose words from the box to complete the paragraph.

canyons	continents	delta	lakes
mesas	mountains	oceans	rivers

Example: Asia and Africa are _____ continents _____.

Earth's surface contains many kinds of land. (1) _____ are very

tall. Some are more than 8,000 meters in height. (2) _____ are not

as tall and they have flat tops. (3) _____ are long, narrow valleys

with steep sides. Earth also has many bodies of water. (4) _____ are

bodies of water that flow from one place to another. They can be very long. You

might see a low area of land called a(n) (5) _____ where a river

ends. (6) _____ are huge bodies of salty water that are very deep.

Their deepest parts can be more than 10,000 meters deep. (7) _____

are much smaller bodies of water. They are found all over Earth's surface and are

good places to swim and fish.

EARTH SCIENCE Earth's Surface • **CONCEPTS**

C WATER ON EARTH

Reading Strategy *Main Idea and Details*

Read **Water on Earth** on page 136 of your student book. Then complete the chart with details that support the main idea.

> **Main Idea and Details**
> ✓ The main idea of a paragraph is the big idea.
> ✓ Details support the main idea.

Main Idea: More than two-thirds of Earth's surface is covered by water.
Detail
Detail
Detail
Detail
Detail

D EARTH'S LANDFORMS

Reading Strategy *Summarizing*

Read **Earth's Landforms** on page 136 of your student book. Write a summary below.

> **Summarizing**
> ✓ Write something in a shorter form.

_____

_____

_____

_____

E SCIENCE SKILL Reading a Topographic Map

Look at the topographic map on page 136 of your student book. Then use words from the box to complete the sentences.

> **Reading a Topographic Map**
> ✓ A topographic map shows the shape and height of a landform.

elevation	~~four~~	higher	hills	lower

Example: The map has _____ four _____ contour lines.

1. The _____ of Coconut Hill is between 20 and 30 meters.

2. Sunset Beach is at a _____ elevation than Palm Tree Point.

3. Palm Tree Point is at a _____ elevation than Coconut Hill.

4. There are two _____ on Sailboat Island.

F FRESH WATER MEETS SALT WATER

Pairwork

Work with a partner to find information about the Mississippi River delta. Then answer the questions below.

1. How large is the Mississippi River delta? Is most of the delta land or water?

   _____

2. Is the delta getting larger or smaller? Why? _____

   _____

   _____

G WRITING Hypothesizing

What landforms are in your state? Choose one and describe it. Then hypothesize what you think created it and why. Write a paragraph.

> **Hypothesizing**
> ✓ Tell what you think happened. Give reasons to support your idea.

_____

_____

_____

_____

LAB **Group Work** River Delta

Question How does a delta form?

Procedure
1. Put 1 scoop each of gravel, sand, potting soil, and peat moss in a jar. Fill the jar 3/4 full with water.
2. Put the lid on the jar. Make sure it is on tight.
3. Hold on to the jar firmly and shake it. Shake the jar for about 1 minute.
4. Set the jar down. Observe what happens to the sand, soil, peat moss, and gravel.

Materials
- jar with lid
- peat moss
- sand
- water
- gravel
- scoop or large spoon
- potting soil

Analysis
1. What did you **observe** when you stopped shaking the jar?

_____

_____

_____

2. What happens to the soil, sand, and rock in a river when the river slows?

_____

_____

📖 Student book pages 138–139

A **VOCABULARY WORDS**

Circle the word or words that complete each sentence.

Example: Most earthquakes occur at (faults) / craters.

1. Earth's crust is divided into blocks of rock called plates / faults.

2. A mountain that forms at an opening in Earth's crust is a(n)

    earthquake / volcano.

3. The focus / epicenter is the place inside Earth where an earthquake starts.

4. Underwater earthquakes cause huge water waves called

    seismic waves / tsunamis.

5. Hot melted rock inside Earth is called magma / lava.

6. A large hole in the ground that may be caused by a volcano is a vent / crater.

B **VOCABULARY IN CONTEXT**

Choose words from the box to complete the paragraph.

seismic waves	~~volcano~~	focus	tsunami
earthquake	faults	epicenter	plates

Example: A _____volcano_____ erupts when melted rock and gases reach Earth's

   surface.

Earth's crust is covered with large (1) _____. Sometimes they

move past each other along cracks in the surface called (2) _____.

This may cause a violent shaking in the crust called a(n) (3) _____.

The shaking is caused by (4) _____ traveling through the inside of

Earth. They can be powerful enough to knock down buildings. The place where an

earthquake starts is called the (5) _____. The place on the surface

above this location is called the (6) _____. If a landslide or an

earthquake occurs on the seafloor it may cause a(n) (7) _____.

📘 Student book pages 140–141

C WHERE DO EARTHQUAKES HAPPEN?

Reading Strategy *Cause and Effect*

Read **Where Do Earthquakes Happen?** on page 140 in your student book. Then answer the questions.

> **Cause and Effect**
> ✓ The cause tells what happens.
> ✓ The effect is the result of the cause.

1. *Cause* What happens when pressure builds up at plate boundaries?

   _____

2. *Effect* What is the result of the plate movement? _____

   _____

D SURFACE WAVES AND TSUNAMIS

Reading Strategy *Comparing and Contrasting*

Read the paragraph. Use it to complete the diagram.

> **Comparing and Contrasting**
> ✓ Tell how things are alike (compare).
> ✓ Tell how things are different (contrast).

Most surface waves on the ocean occur when wind energy moves over the water. A tsunami gets its energy from an earthquake on the sea floor. All earthquakes produce seismic waves. The energy moves out from the earthquake focus in all directions. Some of it reaches the ocean surface. A huge wave forms in the water. It crashes over the land. Tsunamis travel much faster than surface waves. They cause great damage.

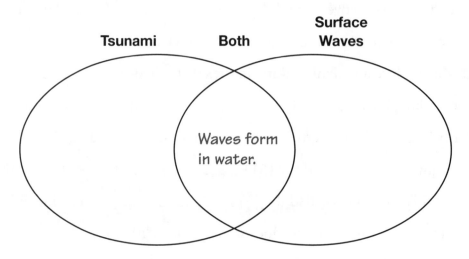

Tsunami   Both   Surface Waves

Waves form in water.

E SCIENCE SKILL Interpreting a Drawing

Read the paragraph below. Then look at the drawing. Answer the questions.

Sometimes earthquakes happen below the sea floor. The shaking of the sea floor produces a lot of energy. All the water above the epicenter is affected. A huge wave forms. When the wave hits the shore, it crashes over the land.

1. Where is the focus of the earthquake in the drawing?

   _____

2. Where is the epicenter of the earthquake in the drawing?

   _____

3. What produces the huge wave? _____

   _____

Interpreting a Drawing

✓ A drawing shows you information. It can help you understand something you have read about.

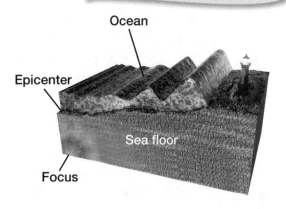

Ocean

Epicenter

Sea floor

Focus

F WHERE DO VOLCANOES FORM?

Pairwork

Work with a partner. Do research on the internet. Find out where volcanoes form in North America. Find out why volcanoes form there. Write two sentences.

_____

_____

_____

G WRITING Making Observations

Imagine you observe an erupting volcano from a safe distance. What do you think you see and feel? Write a paragraph.

Making Observations

✓ Look at something closely to learn about it.

_____

_____

_____

_____

LAB **Group Work** Moving Plates

Question How do Earth's plates move?

Procedure

1. Roll the clay until it is soft enough to mold. Shape the model clay into two bricks about 20 cm long x 10 cm wide x 5 cm thick. Place each brick at the edge of a sheet of foil.

2. Push the bricks tightly together as shown in picture A. Then move them in the direction of the arrows. Are the plates pushing together, pulling apart, or just moving past each other?

_____

3. Fix the shape of the bricks as needed. Place the long side of the bricks along the edge of the foil. Place them tightly together as shown in picture B. Move the bricks in the direction of the arrows. Allow them to slide against each other. Observe and describe what happens.

_____

_____

> **Materials**
> • modeling clay molded into 2 bricks
> • 2 sheets of aluminum foil larger than the bricks
> • dowel rod or thick pencil
> • metric ruler

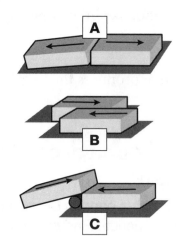

4. Fix the shape of the bricks as needed. Place them as shown in picture C. Use the dowel rod or a thick pencil to lift one clay brick over the other. One brick should be tilted up so it rests on the dowel. Slide the bricks toward each other in the direction of the arrows. Observe and describe what happens.

_____

Analysis

1. What are the ways that Earth's plates can move? Write your **conclusion**.

_____

_____

A VOCABULARY WORDS

Match the items on the left with the correct definitions.

Example: 8. erosion   _8_ the carrying of sediment to new places

1. glacier   ____ a hill formed by a glacier

2. weathering   ____ formed when a river carries sediment to its mouth

3. deposition   ____ breaks rocks into tiny pieces

4. moraine   ____ can be carried away by wind and water

5. delta   ____ caused when water freezes in cracks in rock

6. soil   ____ a mass of moving ice

7. ice wedging   ____ when sediment is dropped in a place

B VOCABULARY IN CONTEXT

Choose words from the box to complete the paragraph.

moraine	~~abrasion~~	sand dune	delta
glacier	deposition	erosion	

Example: Tiny bits of rock blown by the wind can cause _____*abrasion*_____.

Earth's surface can be changed through (1) _____, when wind,

water, and ice carry soil away. For example, a(n) (2) _____ is a huge

section of ice that moves down a mountain. It can carry away pieces of rock and

leave behind a(n) (3) _____. Rivers carry sediment. Through the

process of (4) _____, sediment builds up in an area. This can form

a river (5) _____. Wind can carry soil and sand. Sometimes it is

deposited to form a(n) (6) _____.

📖 Student book pages 144–145

C WEATHERING

Reading Strategy *Summarizing*

Read **Weathering** on page 144 of your student book. Write a summary below.

> **Summarizing**
> ✓ Write something in a shorter form.

_____

_____

_____

_____

D GLACIERS

Reading Strategy *Making Inferences*

Read **Glaciers** on page 144 of your student book. Then decide if each statement below is true or false. Circle **T** for true. Circle **F** for false. Correct the false sentences.

> **Making Inferences**
> ✓ Use what you know to make a decision.

1. Glaciers form during one winter. T or F

_____

2. Glaciers move down mountains. T or F

_____

3. Ice in a glacier wears down mountains. T or F

_____

4. Glaciers form when snow and ice build up. T or F

_____

E **SCIENCE SKILL** Recognizing Cause and Effect

Read the paragraph and look at the picture. Then answer the questions.

Plants will grow in cracks of rocks where they find water and nutrients. With time the plants grow larger and larger. The plants' roots also grow thicker. As the roots grow thicker, they push outward on the rock. Eventually, the rock splits apart.

1. What causes the plant root to push on the rock?

_____

_____

2. What effect does the plant root have on the rock?

_____

F **EROSION AND DEPOSITION**

Pairwork

Work with a partner. Read **Erosion and Deposition** on page 145 of your student book. Then answer the questions.

1. How are erosion and deposition alike? _____

_____

2. How are they different? _____

_____

G **WRITING** Looking for Patterns

Nancy went on vacation in Alaska. She saw a moraine left by a glacier. She saw a wide river delta. She also saw sand dunes on a beach. What do the moraine, delta, and dunes have in common? Write a paragraph.

Looking for Patterns

✓ Look for something that happens again and again.

_____

_____

_____

_____

LAB **Group Work** Glacier Models

Question How do glaciers cut into rock?

Procedure

1. Place several handfuls of golf-ball-sized rocks into the pie tin. Spread the rocks out evenly.
2. Fill the pie tin with water. Do not let the water rise higher than the rocks.
3. Carefully place the pie tin in a freezer. Keep the tin in the freezer until the water has completely frozen. When the water has frozen, take the pie tin out of the freezer.
4. Put the black construction paper flat on a desk or table. Turn the pie tin over so that it is upside down. Place it on one end of the construction paper.
5. Hold the construction paper down. Have your partner slowly push the tin across the paper, from one end to the other. Do this three times.

Materials
- empty pie tin
- several handfuls of golf-ball-sized rocks
- water
- freezer
- large piece of black construction paper

Analysis

1. What happened to the paper as the pie tin moved across it?

   _____

2. What might have happened to the paper if the pie tin was twice as heavy and the rocks were sharper?

   _____

   _____

3. What do your **observations** tell you about rocks and glaciers?

   _____

   _____

A VOCABULARY WORDS

Part 1

Draw a line from each word to the phrase that tells about it.

1. cloud   **a.** air that blows over Earth

2. rain   **b.** what we breathe

3. wind   **c.** oxygen or nitrogen

4. gas   **d.** tiny drops of water that float high in the sky

5. air   **e.** water that falls to the ground in drops

Part 2

Choose three words from the list above. Use each word in a sentence.

Example: Nitrogen is a gas in air.

1. _____

2. _____

3. _____

B VOCABULARY IN CONTEXT

Choose words from the box to complete the paragraph.

air	atmosphere	clouds	rain	fog
particles	pollution	~~wind~~	water vapor	gases

Example: Moving air causes _____wind_____ to blow.

The air around Earth is the (1) _____. (2) _____

is made of several (3) _____ that plants and animals need. Weather,

such as (4) _____ and (5) _____, is found in the

lowest layer of the atmosphere. White (6) _____ form in the sky.

They form from (7) _____. Smoke from factories and

(8) _____ in air can cause (9) _____. This can make it

hard for some people to breathe.

C GASES IN THE ATMOSPHERE

Reading Strategy *Using What You Know*

Think what you know about Earth's atmosphere. Write it in the chart. Then read **Gases in the Atmosphere** on page 148 in your student book. Write what you learned in the chart.

> **Using What You Know**
> ✓ Think what you already know about the topic.
> ✓ Use what you already know to help you understand new information.

What You Know
What You Learned

D THE OXYGEN-CARBON DIOXIDE CYCLE

Reading Strategy *Cause and Effect*

Look at the diagram of **The Oxygen-Carbon Dioxide Cycle** on page 148 of your student book. Use it to complete the chart.

> **Cause and Effect**
> ✓ The cause tells what happened.
> ✓ The effect is the result of the cause.

Cause ➡	Effect
Half the plants on Earth die.	The amount of oxygen in Earth's atmosphere would be cut in half.
The number of plants growing on Earth doubles.	1.
Half the animals on Earth die.	2.

E **SCIENCE SKILL** **Reading a Pie Chart**

Not all planets have atmospheres like Earth. They have different amounts of gases. The pie chart shows the gases in Venus's atmosphere. Use the pie chart to answer the questions.

1. What is the most common gas?

   _____

2. What percent of the atmosphere is nitrogen?

   _____

3. What is one trace gas?

   _____

Atmosphere of Venus

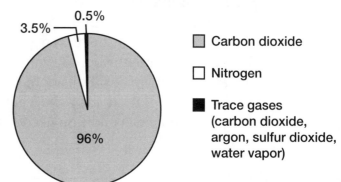

0.5%

3.5%

96%

☐ Carbon dioxide

☐ Nitrogen

■ Trace gases (carbon dioxide, argon, sulfur dioxide, water vapor)

F **LAYERS OF THE ATMOSPHERE**

Pairwork

Read **Layers of the Atmosphere** on page 149 of your student book. Then write two questions. Trade questions with a partner. Answer your partner's two questions.

Question: Which layer is closest to Earth?

Answer: The troposphere is closest to Earth.

G **WRITING** **Making Inferences**

How are people important parts of the oxygen-carbon dioxide cycle? Write a paragraph.

_____

_____

_____

_____

_____

LAB **Group Work** Cloud in a Bottle

Question How do clouds form?

Procedure

1. Fill the bottom of a clear bottle with 1–2 cm of hot tap water. Replace the cap.

2. Shake the bottle strongly for about a minute. Water vapor will mix with the air in the bottle.

3. Place the sheet of construction paper behind the bottle. Squeeze the bottle and then let go. **Observe** what happens. Talk about what you saw with your group. Then, (a) write what you saw, and (b) list the first condition needed for clouds to form below.

Materials
- 2-liter clear plastic bottle and cap (label removed)
- water
- black construction paper
- matches

a. _____

b. _____

4. Lay the bottle on its side. Ask your teacher to light a match for your group. Let it burn for a few seconds and then blow it out.

   Safety Note: Adult help needed. Wait for your teacher to light the matches.

5. Quickly take the cap off the bottle. Hold the burnt match near the opening of the bottle. Let the smoke go inside the bottle. You may push down on the bottle and then let go to help suck the smoke inside.

6. Put the cap back on the bottle. Gently move the bottle back and forth a few times. The water will wash the smoke into the water. Talk about this last step with your group. What do you think is the second condition needed to form a cloud? Write your prediction.

   _____

   _____

7. Place the black construction paper behind the bottle. Squeeze the bottle hard and then let go. What forms inside the bottle? Talk about your observations.

Analysis

1. How is what you saw like a cloud in the sky? _____

   _____

2. What two things are needed for clouds? Write your **conclusion**.

   _____

Gateway to Science Workbook • Copyright © Heinle, Cengage Learning

A VOCABULARY WORDS

Circle the word or words that complete each sentence.

Example: A (warm front) / cold front brings warmer air to an area.

1. Rain and snow are both kinds of precipitation / clouds.

2. Fronts / Weather maps are places where air masses meet.

3. Rain / Water vapor is shown on a weather map.

4. The speed of wind / fog can be measured.

5. Hail / Rain falls as balls of ice.

B VOCABULARY IN CONTEXT

Choose words from the box to complete the paragraph.

air masses	fog	precipitation	snow
~~temperature~~	warm front	weather map	wind

Example: Weather reports tell what the _____temperature_____ is today and whether

it is hot or cold.

Many people watch television news so that they can see the weather

report. The weather report uses a big (1) _____ to show people

what the weather will be like. Most of the time, weather is caused by

(2) _____ that move into an area. For example, when a cold front

moves in, the weather report may tell people that there will be rain,

(3) _____, or other kinds of (4) _____. If a(n)

(5) _____ is coming, the weather report may say that the weather

will be warm and sunny. The weather report also tells the speed of the

(6) _____. Sometimes, if there is (7) _____, the

weather report tells people it will be hard to see when they drive to work.

C WEATHER MAPS

Reading Strategy *Summarizing*

Read **Weather Maps** on page 152 in your student book. Write a summary below.

> **Summarizing**
> ✓ Write something in a shorter form.

_____

_____

_____

_____

_____

D HOW DO CLOUDS AND RAIN FORM?

Reading Strategy *Cause and Effect*

Read **How Do Clouds and Rain Form?** on page 152 in your student book. Then write effects of the causes in the chart.

> **Cause and Effect**
> ✓ The cause is what happened.
> ✓ The effect is the result of the cause.

Cause ➡	Effect
Warm, moist air rises and expands.	The air becomes colder.
Droplets collect around dust or salt particles and come together.	1.
Inside a cloud, droplets bump into one another.	2.
Gravity acts on a heavy droplet.	3.

E SCIENCE SKILL Reading a Weather Map

Look at the weather map and map key on page 151 in your student book. Use it to circle the correct word to complete each sentence.

Example: The highest temperatures are shown in

blue / (purple.)

1. There is a low / high near the center of the United States.

2. One / Two cold fronts are shown on the map.

3. The coldest temperatures on the map are in the 70s / 30s.

4. There are four / two areas of thunderstorms on the map.

F WEATHER AND CLIMATE

Pairwork

Work with a partner. Find your state on the map of climate areas on page 153 in your student book. Then use the internet to find answers to the questions below.

1. What climate area is your state in? _____

_____

2. What kind of weather does your climate have in summer and winter?

_____

3. What precipitation does your climate get? _____

_____

G WRITING Interpreting Information

Your friend lives in a different state. She writes you and says that the weather there has been bad because there have been many low-pressure air masses this summer. Interpret her information to describe what the weather is like where she lives. Write a paragraph.

_____

_____

_____

_____

LAB **Group Work** Predicting the Weather

Question How accurate is the weather forecast?

Procedure

1. Read or watch the weather forecast for 4 days in a row. Record each day's forecast in the chart.

	Sunny or Cloudy	Precipitation	Wind	High Temperature
Day 1				
Day 2				
Day 3				
Day 4				

Materials
- outdoor thermometer
- weather forecast from newspaper (or television)

2. Observe the weather for the same 4 days. Use the temperature from the warmest part of the day. This is usually in the early afternoon. Record your observations in the chart.

	Sunny or Cloudy	Precipitation	Wind	High Temperature
Day 1				
Day 2				
Day 3				
Day 4				

Analysis

1. **Compare** each day's predictions to your **observations.**

_____

_____

2. Which parts of the weather seem most difficult to **predict?** Why?

_____

_____

A VOCABULARY WORDS

Draw a line from each word to the phrase that tells about it.

1. tornado
2. lightning
3. hail
4. waterspout
5. hurricane
6. flood

a. an overflow of water on dry land

b. a small rotating storm that forms over water

c. a rotating column of moist air that touches the ground

d. an electric flash of light in the air

e. a large storm that forms over warm ocean water

f. small balls of ice that fall from the sky like rain

B VOCABULARY IN CONTEXT

Choose words from the box to complete the paragraph.

water vapor	~~thunderstorm~~	tornadoes	lightning
downdraft	updraft	hail	

Example: A ___thunderstorm___ forms when warm, moist air rises into the atmosphere.

Moist air has a lot of (1) _____ in it. As a(n)

(2) _____ carries the warm, moist air higher, it begins to cool. As the

water vapor in the air cools, it forms drops of rain or freezes into balls of

(3) _____. A(n) (4) _____ carries the rain back to

Earth. Noisy thunder and bright flashes of (5) _____ are often part

of a thunderstorm. Rotating columns of moist air that touch the ground are called

(6) _____. They can form in strong thunderstorms.

📖 Student book pages 156–157

C HOW TORNADOES FORM

Reading Strategy *Asking Questions*

Read **How Tornadoes Form** on page 156 in your student book. Write questions and answers about the reading to check your understanding.

> **Asking Questions**
> ✓ When you read, ask yourself questions to check your understanding.
> ✓ Use words like <u>what,</u> <u>where,</u> <u>when,</u> <u>why,</u> and <u>how</u> to form these questions.

Question	Answer
What is a tornado?	a spinning column of moist air that touches the ground

D STAGES OF A HURRICANE

Reading Strategy *Classifying Information*

Read **Stages of a Hurricane** on page 156 in your student book. Use the chart below to classify the stages of a hurricane.

> **Classifying Information**
> ✓ Place information into groups.

Wind Speed	Stage
storm over ocean; low winds; no rotation	Tropical disturbance
winds less than 62 km/h with some rotation	1.
winds between 62 km/h and 117 km/h	2.
winds reach 117 km/h or more	3.

E SCIENCE SKILL Interpreting a Model

Look at the thunderstorm model on pages 154–155 in your student book. Then read the paragraph below and answer the questions.

> **Interpreting a Model**
> ✓ A model is a small version of something.
> ✓ A model shows how something works.

   An updraft carries warm, moist air away from the ground into a cloud. As the cloud rises, it meets icy cold air, and the water vapor cools to form raindrops or hail. Strong downdrafts carry the rain and hail back to Earth.

1. What kind of winds carry the warm air higher into the sky? _____

2. What kind of winds send rain and hail falling toward the ground? _____

   _____

3. What causes rain and hail to form inside the cloud? _____

   _____

F WATCHES AND WARNINGS

Pairwork

Work with a partner. Do research to answer the questions about severe weather.

1. What kinds of severe weather does your area have? _____

   _____

2. How do people in your area get warnings when this kind of weather has been seen?

   _____

3. What should you do when there is a warning? _____

   _____

G WRITING Analyzing Information

You work for a radio station. You write severe-weather warnings. Write a warning that includes this information: Where is the storm? How long will it last? What should people do?

> **Analyzing Information**
> ✓ Study information to understand what it means.

_____

_____

_____

_____

LAB **Group Work** Weather Spinner

Question How do hurricanes start?

Procedure

1. Turn on the light. Turn the light so that it points up. Leave it on for a few minutes, until it becomes warm.

   Safety Note: Do not touch the lightbulb. It may be hot.

2. Cut off the edges of a paper plate. Keep the flat center circle.

   Safety note: Be careful when you use the scissors.

3. Cut a 45-cm long piece of thread. Tape one end to the center of the circle. Use a pen to make a large spiral on the circle.

4. Cut around the spiral you drew. Start cutting at the point where the thread is taped.

5. Hold on to the other end of the thread. The circle should hang flat. Do not let it touch anything.

6. Now hold the circle about 10 cm above the lightbulb. Do not let it touch the bulb. Observe what starts to happen to the paper circle.

Materials
- paper plate
- pen
- tape
- thread (at least 45 cm long)
- scissors
- desk lamp with an incandescent bulb and bendable neck

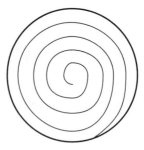

Step 3

Step 5: Finished weather spinner

Analysis

1. What did you **observe** when you held the paper circle over the lightbulb? Why do you think this happened?

   _____

   _____

2. Hurricanes usually start over warm ocean water. Explain how the lightbulb and paper circle modeled the way a hurricane starts.

   _____

   _____

   _____

A VOCABULARY WORDS

Circle the word or words that complete each sentence.

Example: Water energy / (Geothermal energy) comes from inside Earth.

1. Coal is a fossil fuel / mineral.

2. A sailboat uses natural gas / wind energy to move.

3. A dam uses solar energy / water energy to produce electricity.

4. An atomic energy plant produces nuclear energy / solar energy.

5. Gold is a type of fossil fuel / mineral found inside Earth.

6. Newspapers can be recycled / thrown away to save natural resources.

7. Solar energy / Geothermal energy is created by the sun.

B VOCABULARY IN CONTEXT

Choose words from the box to complete the paragraph.

solar energy	wind energy	petroleum
recycle	water energy	geothermal energy
~~minerals~~	natural resources	fossil fuels

Example: Gold, copper, and other _____minerals_____ can be found in Earth's crust.

Energy is one of our most important (1) _____. Natural gas and

(2) _____ are used to make energy. These energy sources are

(3) _____. They come from dead plants and animals. It takes

millions of years for them to form inside Earth's crust. We also get energy from

other sources. Sunlight is used to provide (4) _____. A geyser

produces (5) _____. It uses heat from inside Earth. Many dams have

been built to provide (6) _____. In some areas, strong breezes can

provide (7) _____. It is important to use natural resources wisely.

One way to conserve those resources is to (8) _____.

C RENEWABLE AND NONRENEWABLE RESOURCES

Reading Strategy *Using What You Know*

Think about what you know about natural resources. Write it in the chart. Then read **Renewable and Nonrenewable Resources** on page 160 of your student book. Write what you learned in the chart.

Using What You Know

✓ Think what you already know about the topic.

✓ Use what you already know to help you understand new information.

What You Know
Natural resources are useful materials found in nature.

What You Learned

D RECYCLE, REDUCE, AND REUSE

Reading Strategy *Facts and Examples*

Read **Recycle, Reduce, and Reuse** on page 160 of your student book. Find facts about conserving resources and write them in the chart. Think of examples of the facts.

Facts and Examples

✓ Write down facts as you read.

✓ Write down an example for each fact.

Fact	Example
It is important to conserve natural resources.	It will take millions of years for more fossil fuels to form.

Gateway to Science Workbook • Copyright © Heinle Cengage Learning

E **SCIENCE SKILL Using Percentages**

Use the pie chart to answer the questions below.

1. Which type of energy accounts for 7% of our energy use? _____

2. Which natural resource provides most of our energy? _____

3. What percentage of energy is provided by natural gas? _____

4. What percentage of energy is hydroelectric, solar, and geothermal?

_____

Energy Use in Developed Countries

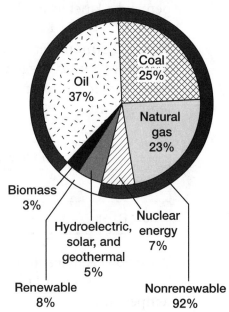

F **WIND FARMS**

Pairwork

Read **Wind Farms** on page 160 of your student book. Work with a partner. Make a list of reasons to use wind energy. Then make a list of reasons why wind energy might not be the best choice.

Reasons to use wind energy:

1. _____

2. _____

3. _____

Reasons not to use wind energy:

4. _____

5. _____

6. _____

G **WRITING Comparing and Contrasting**

How are fossil fuels and biomass the same? How are they different? Write a paragraph to compare and contrast these natural resources.

_____

_____

_____

LAB **Group Work** Solar Energy

Question How do we get energy from the sun?

Procedure

1. Cover the insides of 2 bowls with aluminum foil. Fill the bowls with water. Use the marking pen and a label to mark the bowls as Bowl A and Bowl B.
2. Place a thermometer in each bowl. After 5 minutes, record the temperature of each bowl. Record the temperatures as the beginning temperatures.

Materials
- 2 bowls
- 2 thermometers
- sticky label
- water
- aluminum foil
- marking pen

	Beginning Temperature	Ending Temperature
Bowl A		
Bowl B		

3. Place Bowl A in a sunny place. Leave Bowl B alone.
4. After 2 hours, record the temperature of each bowl. These are the ending temperatures.

Analysis

1. How did the beginning and ending temperatures of Bowl A **compare?** How did the beginning and ending temperatures of Bowl B **compare?**

_____

_____

2. **Draw a conclusion** about how we get energy from the sun.

_____

_____

3. **Predict** what would happen if you did this activity at night.

_____

_____

A VOCABULARY WORDS

Circle the word or words that complete each sentence.

Example: Water vapor is a liquid /(gas.)

1. You get information about the world through your states / senses.

2. Burning and rusting are examples of states / chemical changes.

3. Ice is an example of a liquid / solid.

4. When you touch something, you feel its texture / color.

5. Some foods have a very strong odor / texture.

6. An iron nail can burn / rust.

7. Property can mean a characteristic / gas.

B VOCABULARY IN CONTEXT

Choose words from the box to complete the paragraph.

taste	states	odor	gas	~~chemical changes~~
texture	liquid	color	senses	solid

Example: Burning is a(n) ___chemical change___.

Matter is all around you. You get information about matter through your

(1) _____. Your eyes see (2) _____ and your nose

smells (3) _____. Your fingers feel (4) _____ and

your mouth can (5) _____. Matter can be in three

(6) _____. Matter can be a(n) (7) _____, like a

ball, a block of wood, or a tire. Matter can be a(n) (8) _____, like

milk, juice, or oil. Matter can also be a(n) (9) _____, like the air.

Sometimes matter will change from one state to another.

📖 Student book pages 164–165

C STATES OF MATTER

Reading Strategy *Facts and Examples*

Read **States of Matter** on page 164 in your student book. Write two facts and examples in the chart.

> **Facts and Examples**
> ✓ Write down facts as you read.
> ✓ Write down an example of each fact.

Fact	Example
A solid has a definite shape.	The shape of my desk does not change.

D OBSERVING MATTER

Reading Strategy *Drawing Conclusions*

Different objects have different properties. Read the properties listed in the charts. Then draw a conclusion about what object is described.

> **Drawing Conclusions**
> ✓ Make a decision after you think about all the facts.

Facts	Conclusion
1. The object is: • long • pointed at both ends • yellow • fruity smelling	The object is a(n) _____.
2. The object is: • round • black and white • smooth • filled with air	The object is a(n) _____.
3. The object is: • long • round • made of wax • made to burn	The object is a(n) _____.

E **SCIENCE SKILL** Interpreting an Illustration

Look at the illustration. Then answer the questions.

Solid   Liquid   Gas

1. In which state do the particles spread out evenly to fill the container?

   _____

2. Does liquid have its own shape? How can you tell? _____

   _____

3. Describe the particles that make up a solid. _____

   _____

F **PHYSICAL AND CHEMICAL PROPERTIES**

Pairwork

Read **Physical and Chemical Properties** on page 165 in your student book. Then look at the properties of aluminum. List ways we use the properties of aluminum.

Properties of Aluminum	Uses of Aluminum
• It is very light. • It can be stretched easily. • It does not rust.	used to make soda cans

G **WRITING** Interpreting Information

Iron is a metal. One property is that it is hard and strong. How do we use this property? What things are made of iron? Write a paragraph.

_____

_____

_____

_____

LAB **Group Work** Observing Properties

Question What are an object's properties?

Procedure

1. Observe the nail. Notice its color and shape. Is it hard or soft? Write three words that describe the nail's properties.

   _____

2. Observe the screw. Study the screw's hardness, color, and shape. What are three words that describe the screw's properties?

   _____

3. Use a magnifying glass and your senses to observe the properties of salt. **Do not** taste the salt. What is the shape of one grain of salt? What are two other properties of salt?

   _____

   _____

4. Use your senses to learn the properties of a cotton ball. Write three words you can use to describe the cotton ball's properties.

   _____

> **Materials**
> • nail
> • screw
> • spoonful of salt
> • cotton ball
> • magnifying glass

Analysis

1. **Compare and contrast** the properties of the screw and the nail. How are they alike? How are they different?

   _____

   _____

   _____

2. **Compare and contrast** the properties of the salt and the cotton ball. What properties do they have that are the same? Which properties are different?

   _____

   _____

   _____

A VOCABULARY WORDS

Match the items on the left with the correct definitions.

Example: 8. float   _8_ stay on the surface of a liquid

1. volume   ____ the amount of matter in an object

2. mass   ____ matter that has definite shape and volume

3. gas   ____ the temperature at which something melts

4. liquid   ____ matter that has a definite volume but no shape

5. melting point   ____ the amount of space something occupies

6. freezing point ____ matter that is neither solid nor liquid

7. solid   ____ the temperature at which something freezes

B VOCABULARY IN CONTEXT

Choose words from the box to complete the paragraphs.

boiling point	float	freezing point	volume	sink
graduated cylinder	~~liquid~~	thermometer	mass	

Example: When ice reaches its melting point, it becomes a _____liquid_____.

Scientists use different tools to measure matter. The tool they use depends on what they want to know. If they want to know (1) _____, they use a balance. If they want to know the (2) _____ of a liquid, they use a (3) _____. If they want to measure how hot something is, they use a (4) _____. The temperature at which a liquid boils is called the (5) _____. The temperature at which a liquid freezes is the (6) _____.

Scientists can tell if an object will (7) _____ or (8) _____ by dropping it into a liquid. Then, they watch to see if it stays on the surface or drops below it.

C CHANGES OF STATE

Reading Strategy *Inferring from Evidence*

Read **Changes of State** on page 168 of your student book. Then think about what happens in the kitchen of your home. Answer the questions below.

> **Inferring from Evidence**
> ✓ Make a guess about something from facts you know.

1. What happens if you leave a dish of ice cream on the table? _____

   _____

2. What happens if you put juice in the freezer? _____

   _____

3. What is another change of state that happens in the kitchen? _____

   _____

D BUOYANCY

Reading Strategy *Cause and Effect*

Read **Buoyancy** on page 168 of your student book. Look at the drawing below. Then answer the questions.

> **Cause and Effect**
> ✓ The cause tells what happened.
> ✓ The effect is the result of the cause.

Force of gravity

Buoyant force

1. *Cause* Which force is greater on the log, the force of gravity or the buoyant force?

   _____

2. *Effect* What happens to the log? _____

   _____

E SCIENCE SKILL Using Numbers to Compare

Look at the chart to the right. It shows the melting points of different metals. Use the numbers in the chart to answer the questions.

1. Which two metals have the lowest melting points?

   _____

2. How much higher than the melting point of aluminum is the melting point of iron?

   _____

3. How much lower is the melting point of silver than the melting point of gold?

   _____

Metal	Melting point
Aluminum	660°C
Gold	1,063°C
Iron	1,593°C
Lead	327°C
Silver	961°C
Tin	232°C

F MASS, VOLUME, AND DENSITY
Pairwork

Work with a partner. Use a balance to find the mass of a wooden or plastic block. Then use a metric ruler to measure the length, width, and height of the block in centimeters. Multiply length × width × height to find the volume of the block in cubic centimeters. Finally divide the block's mass by its volume to find the density. Record your information in the chart.

Mass of block	
Volume of block (L × W × H)	
Density of block (M ÷ V)	

G WRITING Analyzing Evidence

Juan poured three liquids into a beaker. The liquids formed three layers like the ones in the picture. What did his results tell him about the densities of the three liquids? Write a paragraph.

_____

_____

_____

_____

_____

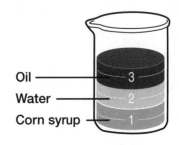

Oil ——— 3
Water ——— 2
Corn syrup ——— 1

LAB **Group Work** Melting Ice

Question Does the mass of ice change when it melts?

Procedure

1. Use the balance to measure the mass of the plastic cup.

_____

2. Fill the cup with ice. Then measure the mass of the cup full of ice. Record your data.

_____

3. Subtract the mass of the cup from the mass of the cup filled with ice. This is the mass of the ice alone. Record your data.

_____

4. Place the cup in a warm place. Let the ice melt completely.

5. Measure the mass of the cup of water. Subtract the mass of the cup from the mass of the cup full of water. This is the mass of the water alone. Record your data.

_____

| **Materials** |
| • plastic cup |
| • several ice cubes |
| • balance |

Analysis

1. What change of state did you **observe** when the ice melted?

_____

2. **Compare** the mass of the ice to the mass of the water.

_____

3. **Infer** what happens to mass when matter changes state.

_____

_____

Name _____ Date _____

📖 Student book pages 170–171

A VOCABULARY WORDS

Label the drawing below.

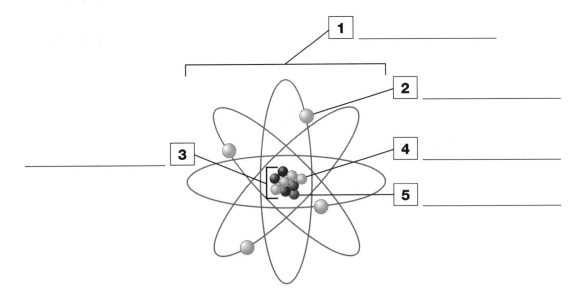

| 1 | _____ |

| 2 | _____ |

3 _____

| 4 | _____ |

| 5 | _____ |

B VOCABULARY IN CONTEXT

Choose words from the box to complete the paragraphs.

| electrons | silver | nonmetals | atoms | ~~oxygen~~ |
| element | gold | protons | neutrons | molecules |

Example: _____ Oxygen _____ is a nonmetal.

The food you eat is matter. Your body is matter. The things around you are

matter. Matter is made up of (1) _____. Atoms are made

of three different particles. These particles are (2) _____,

(3) _____, and (4) _____.

Only one kind of atom is found in a(n) (5) _____. The metals

(6) _____ and (7) _____ are made from two different

atoms. (8) _____, such as carbon, are made from one kind of atom.

(9) _____ are made from two or more atoms.

📖 Student book pages 172–173

C STRUCTURE OF AN ATOM

Reading Strategy *Main Idea and Details*

Read **Structure of an Atom** on page 172 of your student book. Then fill in the chart with details to support the main idea.

Main Idea and Details

✓ The main idea of a paragraph is the big idea.

✓ Details support the main idea.

Main Idea: An atom has three parts.		
Detail	**Detail**	**Detail**

D MOLECULES

Reading Strategy *Asking Questions*

Read **Molecules** on page 172 of your student book. Write questions and answers about the reading to check your understanding.

Asking Questions

✓ When you read, ask yourself questions to check your understanding.

✓ Use words like <u>what</u>, <u>when</u>, <u>where</u>, <u>why</u>, and <u>how</u> to form questions.

Questions	Answers
When does a molecule form?	Molecules form when two or more atoms join together.

170

E SCIENCE SKILL Interpreting a Diagram

The diagram shows an atom.

1. What particles are found in the center of an atom?

   _____

   _____

2. What particle moves around the center of the atom?

   _____

   _____

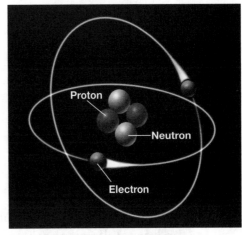

Structure of an Atom

F THE PERIODIC TABLE OF ELEMENTS

Pairwork

Look at the list of elements below. Think where you can find these elements. Write sentences with your partner.

Example: Chlorine (Cl) *Chlorine keeps swimming pools clean.* _____

1. Aluminum (Al) _____

   _____

2. Oxygen (O) _____

   _____

G WRITING Looking for Patterns

Suppose you discover a new element. How will you decide where the element belongs on the periodic table? Write a paragraph to explain.

_____

_____

_____

_____

PHYSICAL SCIENCE · Atoms and Molecules · **LAB**

LAB Group Work Periodic Table

Question What patterns are there in the periodic table?

Procedure

1. Look at the periodic table on pages 222–223 in your student book. What do the boxes tell you about each element?

   _____

   _____

2. Observe any patterns you see as you read across a row. Write your observations.

   _____

   _____

   _____

3. Observe any patterns you see as you read down a column. Write your observations.

   _____

   _____

   _____

4. Compare your observations with other students in your group.

Analysis

1. How are the elements in the periodic table arranged? Write your **conclusion**.

   _____

   _____

Name _____ Date _____

A VOCABULARY WORDS

Complete the crossword.

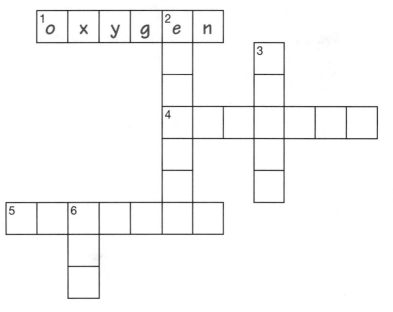

Across

1. ____ is an element.

4. A ____ can be homogeneous or heterogeneous.

5. ____ is a rock that is a heterogeneous mixture.

Down

2. Aluminum is an ____.

3. ____ is a compound that you can drink.

6. ____ is a homogeneous mixture that you breathe.

B VOCABULARY IN CONTEXT

Choose words from the box to complete the paragraph.

pure substances	aluminum	compound	water
mixture	element	air	granite

Example: Elements and compounds are both __pure substances__.

Oxygen is a(n) (1) _____. It is a pure substance that is made of

only one kind of atom. (2) _____ is another element. But

(3) _____ is a compound. A(n) (4) _____ is a pure

substance that is made of two or more elements that are joined together.

A(n) (5) _____ is made of two or more pure substances that are

mixed together. (6) _____ is a mixture of many gases.

(7) _____ is another mixture.

📖 Student book pages 176–177

C COMMON COMPOUNDS

Reading Strategy *Scanning for Information*

Read questions 1–3 below. Then read **Common Compounds** on page 176 in your student book and find the answers.

> **Scanning for Information**
> ✓ Understand what information you need before reading.
> ✓ Read to find the information.

1. What are some common compounds?	
2. How do compounds form?	
3. What elements join to form salt?	

D TYPES OF MIXTURES

Reading Strategy *Inferring from Evidence*

Read **Types of Mixtures** on page 176 in your student book. Then decide if the sentences below are true or false. Circle **T** for true. Circle **F** for false. If the sentence is false, write the correct word or words on the line.

> **Inferring from Evidence**
> ✓ Make a guess about something from facts you know.

Example: A mixture <u>is</u> a pure substance. T or Ⓕ

is not _____

1. Salad dressing forms a <u>homogeneous</u> mixture. T or F

_____

2. You can see the different parts of a <u>suspension</u>. T or F

_____

3. Dissolving salt in water forms a <u>heterogeneous</u> mixture. T or F

_____

4. In a mixture, two or more substances <u>join chemically</u>. T or F

_____

E SCIENCE SKILL Comparing and Contrasting

Study the table and answer the questions.

Compound	State at room temperature	Elements joined in the compound
Carbon dioxide	gas	carbon and oxygen
Table salt	solid	sodium and chlorine
Water	liquid	hydrogen and oxygen
Chalk	solid	calcium, carbon, and oxygen
Ammonia	gas	nitrogen and hydrogen

Comparing and Contrasting
✓ Tell how things are the same (compare).
✓ Tell how things are different (contrast).

1. How are carbon dioxide, water, and chalk the same? _____

_____

2. How are table salt and chalk the same? _____

_____

3. How are ammonia and water different? _____

_____

F PHYSICAL AND CHEMICAL CHANGES

Pairwork

Work with a partner. Read **Physical and Chemical Changes** on page 177 in your student book. Then answer the questions.

1. What happens during a physical change? Think of an example.
2. What happens during a chemical change? Think of an example.

G WRITING Making Inferences

You use a match to light a candle. After an hour, some of the candle wax is melted. What was a physical change? What was a chemical change? How do you know? Write a paragraph.

Making Inferences
✓ Use what you know to make a decision.

_____

_____

_____

_____

LAB **Group Work** Separating Mixtures

Question How can you separate mixtures?

Procedure

1. Mix iron filings and sand in a bowl.
2. Put the magnet in the plastic bag. Close the bag. Hold the magnet in the mixture of iron filings and sand. What do you observe?

_____

3. Now put 1 spoonful of salt into the cup of water. Stir until the salt has dissolved. What kind of mixture did you make?

_____

4. Pour the salt water into a shallow pan. Place the pan in a warm, sunny place. Leave it there until the water has evaporated. (This may take a few days.) What do you observe?

   Safety Note: Wash your hands after pouring. Wipe up any spills.

_____

Materials
- bowl
- cup half-filled with water
- sand
- table salt
- iron filings
- plastic spoon
- magnet
- shallow pan
- small zip-top plastic bag

Analysis

1. **Draw a conclusion** about how you can separate a mixture that contains iron.

_____

_____

2. What is one way you can separate the parts of a solution?

_____

_____

3. Suppose you made a mixture of sand and water. **Hypothesize** how you could separate the parts.

_____

_____

A VOCABULARY WORDS

Unscramble the underlined word in each sentence. Write the word on the line.

Example: Water is a(n) <u>mcpudnoo</u>.

_____compound_____

1. A water <u>loecelum</u> is made of hydrogen and oxygen.

_____

2. A(n) <u>notrcele</u> is part of an atom.

_____

3. A(n) <u>toma</u> has a nucleus.

_____

4. Sodium is a(n) <u>menelte</u>.

_____

5. A(n) <u>obdn</u> joins hydrogen and oxygen atoms together.

_____

B VOCABULARY IN CONTEXT

Choose words from the box to complete the paragraph.

molecules	rust	compound	~~burning~~
formula	element	symbol	

Example: _____Burning_____ is a chemical reaction.

(1) _____ are formed when atoms join together.

A(n) (2) _____ forms when the atoms that join are different.

(3) _____ is a compound made up of iron and oxygen atoms. A(n) (4) _____ contains only one type of atom. Every element has a(n) (5) _____, such as O for oxygen and H for hydrogen. A compound's (6) _____ shows the atoms in the compound.

📖 Student book pages 180–181

C CHEMICAL BONDS

Reading Strategy *Main Idea and Details*

Read **Chemical Bonds** on page 180 in your student book. Then complete the table with details that support the main idea.

> **Main Idea and Details**
> ✓ The main idea of a paragraph is the big idea.
> ✓ Details support the main idea.

Main Idea: Chemical reactions break chemical bonds and form new ones.	
Detail Some reactions give off energy.	**Detail**
Detail	**Detail**

D CHEMICAL EQUATIONS

Reading Strategy *Summarizing*

Read **Chemical Equations** on page 180 in your student book. Tell what happens when hydrogen and oxygen join together.

> **Summarizing**
> ✓ Write something in a shorter form.

_____

_____

_____

_____

E SCIENCE SKILL Reading an Equation

Look at the chemical equation. Then answer the questions.

Reading an Equation

✓ In a chemical equation, the reactants are on the left. The product is on the right.

$$C + O_2 \rightarrow CO_2$$

1. What are the reactants in this equation? _____

_____

2. What elements are combined in the product? _____

_____

F CONSERVATION OF MASS

Pairwork

Read **Conservation of Mass** on page 181 in your student book. Then work with a partner to answer the question below.

Iron and oxygen combine to form rust. How would you describe the law of conservation of mass for this reaction?

_____

_____

_____

G WRITING Applying Information

A scientist combines hydrogen and oxygen to form water. The mass of the water is 8 grams. What was the total mass of the hydrogen and oxygen before they combined? How do you know? Write a paragraph.

Applying Information

✓ Use information for a particular reason.

_____

_____

_____

_____

LAB **Group Work** Conservation of Mass

Question Is mass conserved during a chemical reaction?

Procedure

1. Measure 60 milliliters of vinegar. Use one funnel to pour the vinegar into the plastic bottle.
2. Measure 3 grams of baking soda. Use the other funnel to pour the baking soda into the balloon.
3. Attach the balloon to the opening of the bottle. Do not let any baking soda fall into the bottle!
4. Use the balance to measure the mass of the bottle with the balloon attached. Record the mass.

_____

5. Take the bottle off the balance. Carefully dump the baking soda into the bottle. Hold on to the opening of the balloon so it does not slip off the bottle. What do you observe?

_____

_____

6. Do not remove the balloon from the bottle. Put the bottle and balloon on the balance again. Measure the mass. Record the mass.

_____

Materials
- empty plastic water bottle
- baking soda
- 2 small funnels
- balance
- vinegar
- balloon
- 100-mL graduated cylinder

Analysis

1. What were the reactants in this chemical reaction? _____

_____

2. **Compare** the mass before and after you dumped the baking soda into the vinegar.

_____

Name _____ Date _____

📖 Student book pages 182–183

A VOCABULARY WORDS

Circle the word or words that complete each sentence.

Example: Exposure to any kind of concrete / (radiation) can be dangerous.

1. Materials that have an unstable nucleus are called aluminum / radioactive.

2. Alpha particles are the most / least powerful type of radiation.

3. Gamma rays are the most / least powerful type of radiation.

4. Scientists wear special clothing when they work with radioactive samples / radioactive symbols.

5. Concrete / Aluminum foil can block beta particles.

6. Beta particles and gamma rays can pass through aluminum / paper.

B VOCABULARY IN CONTEXT

Choose words from the box to complete the paragraph.

radioactive sample	radioactive symbol	atom
radiation	gamma rays	~~nucleus~~
beta particles	alpha particles	

Example: The center of an atom is called the _____nucleus_____.

Sometimes an (1) _____ gives off particles and energy. These

particles and energy are called (2) _____. The slowest type of

radiation is made up of (3) _____. (4) _____

are smaller and faster. (5) _____ are the most powerful type of

radiation. Scientists wear special clothing when they handle a

(6) _____. Radioactive materials are often marked with a

(7) _____ to warn people of danger.

C DISCOVERY OF RADIOACTIVITY

Reading Strategy *Cause and Effect*

Read **Discovery of Radioactivity** on page 184 in
your student book. Then answer the questions.

Cause and Effect
✓ The cause tells what happened.
✓ The effect is the result of the cause.

1. *Cause* What was put in the drawer with the
   photographic plate?

   _____

2. *Effect* What happened as a result? _____

   _____

D RADIOACTIVE DECAY

Reading Strategy *Main Idea and Details*

Read about **Radioactive Decay** on page 184 of
your student book. Then complete the chart with
details that support the main idea.

Main Idea and Details
✓ The main idea of a paragraph is the big idea.
✓ Details support the main idea.

Main Idea: An atom decays when it gives off particles or energy.		
Detail	**Detail**	**Detail**
An atom can release an alpha particle.		

E SCIENCE SKILL Comparing Data

People are exposed to radiation every day. Radiation comes from natural and human-made sources. The table below shows the main sources of radiation. Use the table to answer the questions.

Comparing Data
✓ Scientists often compare data. Placing data in a table makes the data easier to compare.

Source of Radiation	Natural or Human-Made	Percentage
radon (a gas found in the air)	natural	55%
inside human body	natural	11%
rocks and soil	natural	8%
outer space	natural	8%
consumer products	human-made	3%
medical	human-made	15%

1. What is the source of the most radiation? _____

2. What percentage of a person's contact with radiation comes from medical uses?

   _____

3. What percentage of a person's contact with radiation comes from natural sources?

   _____

F USES OF RADIATION

Pairwork

Work with a partner. Make a list of ways radiation helps people.

G WRITING Applying Information

What is the half-life of carbon-14? What does this mean? How do scientists use carbon-14? Write a paragraph.

Applying Information
✓ Use information for a particular reason.

_____

_____

_____

_____

LAB Group Work Model Half-Life

Question How can you make a model of half-life?

Procedure

1. Put 200 pennies tails up in a shoebox.
2. Put the cover on the box. Then, shake the box with one quick up-and-down motion.
3. Open the box. Remove all pennies that are heads up. These pennies model atoms that decayed.
4. Record the number of pennies removed. Then record the number of pennies left in the box. Use the data table below to organize your data.

Materials
- shoebox with cover
- 200 pennies

Trial	Number of Pennies Removed	Number of Pennies Left in the Box
1		
2		
3		
4		
5		
6		
7		
8		
9		
10		

5. Do steps 2–4 nine more times.

Analysis

1. How many times did you have to shake the box to remove half the pennies?

_____

2. Each shake represents one year. What is the half-life of the atoms?

_____

A VOCABULARY WORDS

Draw a line from each word to the phrase that tells about it.

1. gravity		**a.** no longer moving
2. unbalanced		**b.** a force that moves objects away from you
3. move		**c.** a force that pulls things toward the ground
4. balanced		**d.** when an object's position changes
5. stop		**e.** forces that are equal to each other
6. friction		**f.** a force that moves objects toward you
7. pull		**g.** forces that are not equal to each other
8. push		**h.** the force of objects rubbing against each other

B VOCABULARY IN CONTEXT

Choose words from the box to complete the paragraph.

pull	move	friction	~~gravity~~	push	stop

Example: Earth's _____*gravity*_____ pulls objects to the ground.

Objects (1) _____ all the time. Children push each other on swings. Children pull sleds up a hill. Children slide down the hill on their sleds. Objects move because of forces. One force is a (2) _____. This force makes objects move away from you. Another force is a (3) _____. This force makes objects move toward you. Sometimes objects rub against each other. This causes a force called (4) _____. Friction can make an object (5) _____ moving.

📖 Student book pages 188–189

C **GRAVITY**

Reading Strategy *Cause and Effect*

Read **Gravity** on page 188 in your student book.
Use it to complete the chart.

> **Cause and Effect**
> ✓ The cause tells what happened.
> ✓ The effect is the result of the cause.

Cause	➡	Effect
The sun's gravity pulls on the planets.		1.
Earth has more mass than the moon.		2.

D **FRICTION**

Reading Strategy *Making an Inference*

Read the paragraph below. Then answer the questions.

> **Making an Inference**
> ✓ Use what you know to make a decision.

Friction is a force that happens when two surfaces rub against each other. Friction always opposes motion. When rough surfaces rub against each other, there is a lot of friction. You have to push with more force. When smooth surfaces rub together, there is less friction. You use less force. Using wheels to move something reduces friction. You use even less force.

1. Would it be easier to push a heavy box across a tile floor or across a rug? Why?

_____

_____

2. Would it be easier to move a box by pushing it or pulling it in a wagon? Why?

_____

_____

E **SCIENCE SKILL Using Numbers to Compare**

There are six different coins used in the United States: the penny, nickel, dime, quarter, half-dollar, and dollar. Each of the coins has a different mass. Use the table to answer the questions.

1. Which coin has the greatest mass?

   _____

2. Which coin has the least mass?

   _____

3. Which two coins have almost the same mass?

   _____

> **Using Numbers to Compare**
> ✓ You can use numbers to tell how things are alike and different.

Coin	Mass
penny	2.5 g
nickel	5.0 g
dime	2.268 g
quarter	5.67 g
half-dollar	11.34 g
dollar	8.1 g

F **BALANCED AND UNBALANCED FORCES**

Pairwork

Read **Balanced and Unbalanced Forces** on page 189 in your student book. Work with a partner to think of situations that have balanced or unbalanced forces. Write a sentence to describe each situation.

Example: _Unbalanced: Two children are pushing a door open, and one child is_
pulling the door closed.

1. _____

2. _____

G **WRITING Inferring from Evidence**

Two wrestlers are pushing against each other. How can you tell if the forces are balanced or unbalanced? Write a paragraph.

> **Inferring from Evidence**
> ✓ Make a guess about something from facts you know.

_____

_____

_____

_____

LAB Group Work Falling Objects

Question Do objects fall to the ground at the same speed?

Procedure

1. In this lab you will drop objects to the floor. One person will drop the objects. The other students record what happens.

2. Hold the paper clip in one hand and the pen cap in the other hand. Hold both hands at the same distance from the floor. You will drop these objects at the same time. Predict which object will hit the floor first.

_____

3. Drop the paper clip and pen cap at the same time. Observe what happens. Record the results.

_____

4. Hold the eraser and glue stick. Predict what will happen when you drop them. (a) Record your prediction. Then drop them. Observe what happens. (b) Record the results.

   a. _____

   b. _____

5. Hold the eraser and paper clip. Predict what will happen when you drop them. (a) Record your prediction. Then drop them. Observe what happens. (b) Record the results.

   a. _____

   b. _____

Materials
- paper clip
- chalkboard eraser
- notebook and pencil
- glue stick
- pen cap

Analysis

1. Did the larger objects fall to the ground faster than the smaller objects?

_____

2. What **conclusion** can you draw from this lab about falling objects?

_____

📖 Student book pages 190–191

A VOCABULARY WORDS

Circle the word or words that complete each sentence.

Example: A mass / (force) makes an object move.

1. Acceleration / Velocity is a change in speed or direction.

2. How fast something is moving is the object's mass / speed.

3. Action forces and reaction forces / acceleration always happen in pairs.

4. The speed of a car in a direction is its action force / velocity.

5. It takes more force to change the acceleration of an object with

   large mass / small mass.

B VOCABULARY IN CONTEXT

Choose words from the box to complete the paragraph.

acceleration	force	velocity	~~mass~~	speed

Example: The sun has more _____*mass*_____ than the moon.

   An object moves because of a(n) (1) _____. An object's

(2) _____ tells how fast the object is moving. An object's speed and

direction is its (3) _____. Sometimes a moving object will slow

down or speed up. An object may also change direction. A change in speed or

direction is called (4) _____.

C NEWTON'S FIRST LAW

Reading Strategy *Facts and Examples*

Read **Newton's First Law** on page 192 in your student book. Then complete the chart.

> **Facts and Examples**
> ✓ Write down facts as you read.
> ✓ Write down an example for each fact.

Fact	Examples
An object will stay in motion unless a force acts on it.	1.
	2.
	3.

D NEWTON'S SECOND LAW

Reading Strategy *Inferring from Evidence*

Read **Newton's Second Law** on page 192 in your student book. Then answer the questions.

> **Inferring from Evidence**
> ✓ Make a guess about something from facts you know.

1. Roberto throws a tennis ball to a friend. He then throws a baseball with the same amount of force. Which ball is accelerated more? Why?

   _____

   _____

   _____

2. Think of a waterfall. Water accelerates as it goes over the edge and down toward the ground. Why?

   _____

   _____

   _____

Gateway to Science Workbook • Copyright © Heinle, Cengage Learning

(E) SCIENCE SKILL Using Math to Solve Problems

Newton's second law can be shown with an equation. The equation is $F = m \times a$. In this equation, the F stands for *force* (measured in newtons), the m stands for *mass*, and the a stands for *acceleration*. To use the equation, multiply the mass by the acceleration.

> **Using Math to Solve Problems**
>
> ✓ Many problems about speed, acceleration, and velocity use numbers. You can use math to solve these problems.

1. What is the force if the acceleration is 3 m/s/s and the mass is 7 kg?

   _____

2. What is the force if the acceleration is 9 m/s/s and the mass is 6 kg?

   _____

3. What is the force if the acceleration is 5 m/s/s and the mass is 4 kg?

   _____

4. What is the force if the acceleration is 6 m/s/s and the mass is 8 kg?

   _____

(F) NEWTON'S THIRD LAW

Pairwork

With a partner, think of a situation that shows Newton's third law in action. Write sentences to describe the situation.

Example: Rodrigo is sitting in an office chair on wheels. He pushes against the wall. The chair rolls away from the wall.

_____

_____

_____

(G) WRITING Applying Information

Martin is walking through his room. His foot accidentally hits a toy car on the floor. What happens to the car? Why? Use Newton's first law to explain. Write a paragraph.

> **Applying Information**
>
> ✓ Use information for a particular reason.

_____

_____

_____

_____

LAB **Group Work** The Rolling Tennis Ball

Question How are mass and inertia related?

Procedure

1. Place 2 paperback books on top of one another on the floor. Set a large textbook on top of the books. One end of the textbook should touch the floor to form a ramp.

2. Place the CD case 70 centimeters from the end of the ramp. Use your meter stick to measure the distance. Stand the CD case up on its side.

3. Place the tennis ball at the top of the ramp. Let the ball go so it rolls down the ramp. If the ball does not hit the CD case, roll the ball again. Observe what happens when the ball hits the CD case.

> **Materials**
> • 3 paperback books
> • tennis ball
> • meter stick
> • 2 large textbooks
> • empty CD case

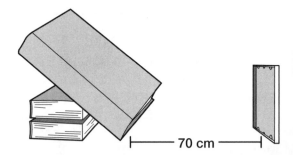

_____

4. Replace the CD case with a paperback book. Stand the book up. Let the ball roll down the ramp again. Observe what happens when the ball hits the paperback.

_____

5. Replace the paperback book with a large textbook. Stand the book up. Again let the ball roll down the ramp. Observe what happens when the ball hits the textbook.

_____

Analysis

1. Which object has the most mass—the CD case, the paperback book, or the textbook?

_____

2. Which object moved the least when it was hit? Which object moved the most?

_____

3. How does an object's mass affect its inertia? _____

_____

A **VOCABULARY WORDS**

Label each picture with a word from the box.

| wheel and axle | pulley | inclined plane | screw |

1. _____

3. _____

2. _____

4. _____

B **VOCABULARY IN CONTEXT**

Choose words from the box to complete the paragraph.

| wedge | ~~inclined plane~~ | lever | pulley | fulcrum | load |

Example: She pushed the rock up an ___inclined plane___.

Simple machines make many tasks easier. These machines can help you

move a heavy (1) _____, tip something over, or break something

apart. Suppose a worker needs to raise a large crate. The crate is heavy, so she

uses a (2) _____, which has a wheel and a rope. Another simple

machine can help you move something heavy. It is a board or rod and is called

a (3) _____. This machine turns on a fixed point, called a

(4) _____. Have you ever had two objects stuck together that you

needed to separate? If so, you might have used a (5) _____. An ax

blade is an example of this kind of simple machine.

📖 Student book pages 196–197

C FORCE AND DISTANCE

Reading Strategy *Comparing and Contrasting*

Read **Force and Distance** on page 196 of your student book. Then look at the picture of the two paths on the hill. Answer the questions.

> **Comparing and Contrasting**
> ✓ Tell how things are the same (compare).
> ✓ Tell how things are different (contrast).

1. How are the two paths similar?

   _____

   _____

2. How are the two paths different?

   _____

3. Which path is easier to walk up? Why? _____

   _____

D THE WEDGE

Reading Strategy *Cause and Effect*

Read **The Wedge** on page 196 of your student book. Then complete the chart.

> **Cause and Effect**
> ✓ The cause tells what happened.
> ✓ The effect is the result of the cause.

Cause	➡	Effect
Effort force was applied to the wedge.		
		The wood split apart.

Gateway to Science Workbook • Copyright © Heinle, Cengage Learning

E SCIENCE SKILL Interpreting a Simple Machine Diagram

You need to move a heavy box onto the stage. Two ramps lead to the stage. Look at the diagram. Then answer the questions.

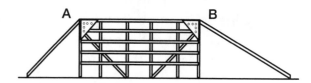

1. Which ramp is longer, Ramp A or Ramp B?

   _____

2. With which ramp would you use the most force? Why?

   _____

   _____

3. Which ramp is easier to use? Why? _____

   _____

F COMPOUND MACHINES

Pairwork

Work with a partner. Use the internet to find other examples of compound machines. Write sentences to describe one other compound machine.

_____

_____

_____

G WRITING Drawing Conclusions

Look at the picture of the wheelbarrow on page 195 of your student book. Is the wheelbarrow a simple machine or a compound machine? How do you know? Does using a wheelbarrow let you do less work to move rocks? Write a paragraph.

_____

_____

_____

_____

LAB **Group Work** Name That Simple Machine

Question What simple machine is being used?

Procedure

1. Place the pencils together so they are side by side. Wrap pieces of tape around the ends of the pencils so that the pencils are stuck together. Do not put tape in the middle of the pencils.

Materials
- 2 unsharpened pencils
- 1 flat toothpick
- 1 screwdriver
- tape

2. Place the pencils on your desk or table. Use your hands to try to separate the two pencils. Try to separate them enough so that your partner can place the toothpick in between them.
3. If you fit the toothpick in, take it out.
4. Place the pencils on the desk or table again. Use the metal tip of the screwdriver to try to separate the pencils. Have your partner place the toothpick between them.

   Safety Note: *Be careful when using the screwdriver. Do not push down on it too hard.*

Analysis

1. Which did a better job of separating the pencils—your hands or the screwdriver?

   _____

2. What kind of simple machine did you use? _____

   _____

3. How did the simple machine work? _____

   _____

   _____

📖 Student book pages 198–199

A VOCABULARY WORDS

Label the diagram of a transverse wave.

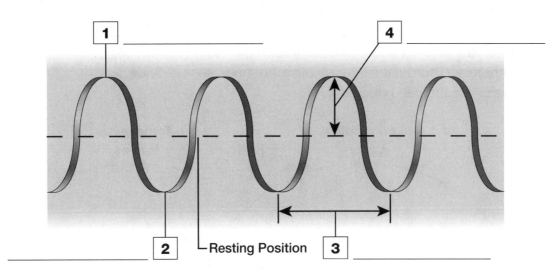

Resting Position

B VOCABULARY IN CONTEXT

Choose words from the box to complete the paragraph.

transverse wave	compression	~~sound wave~~	crest	trough
longitudinal wave	wavelength	rarefaction	waves	amplitude

Example: The distance between two compressions in a ___sound wave___ is the wavelength.

(1) _____ carry energy. A(n) (2) _____ carries energy through water. The highest part of the wave is called the (3) _____. The lowest part of the wave is called the (4) _____. The distance between two crests is the (5) _____. The (6) _____ is the height of the wave. A(n) (7) _____ carries sound energy. Sound energy causes particles in the air to move. A(n) (8) _____ is formed when the particles are pushed together. A(n) (9) _____ is formed when the particles spread out.

C LONGITUDINAL AND TRANSVERSE WAVES

Reading Strategy *Comparing and Contrasting*

Read **Longitudinal and Transverse Waves** on page 200 in your student book. Use the information to compare and contrast longitudinal and transverse waves. Use the Venn diagram.

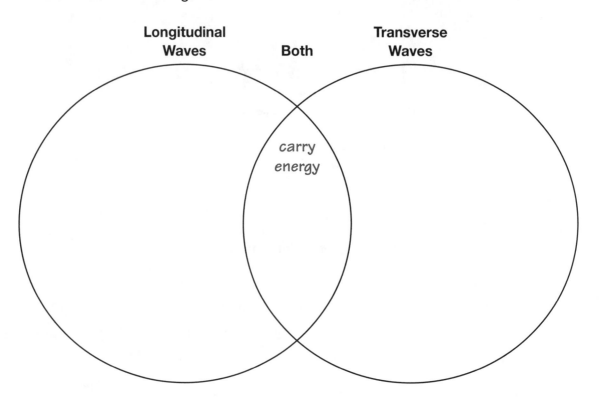

D ELECTROMAGNETIC SPECTRUM

Reading Strategy *Drawing Conclusions*

Read **Electromagnetic Spectrum** on page 201 in your student book. Look at the diagram of the electromagnetic spectrum. Then answer the questions.

1. Do visible light waves have longer or shorter wavelengths than radio waves?

_____

2. Which type of wave has greater energy—microwaves or X-rays?

_____

E SCIENCE SKILL Interpreting a Model

A student uses dominoes to model the way sound energy travels in waves. She sets the dominoes up as shown in the picture.

> **Interpreting a Model**
> ✓ A model can help you visualize how a concept works.

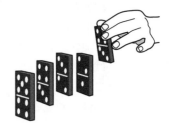

1. What will happen when the student knocks the first domino into the second domino?

   _____

2. What happens to particles in a medium when sound energy travels through it? Is matter carried along by the sound wave?

   _____

   _____

F USES OF ELECTROMAGNETIC WAVES

Pairwork

Read **Uses of Electromagnetic Waves** on page 201 in your student book. Work with a partner. Write different electromagnetic waves in the chart. Use the diagram of the electromagnetic spectrum and the internet to find ways we use the waves.

Electromagnetic Wave	Use
radio waves	send TV signals

G WRITING Comparing and Contrasting

How are microwaves similar to visible light? How are they different? Write a paragraph.

> **Comparing and Contrasting**
> ✓ Tell how things are the same (compare).
> ✓ Tell how things are different (contrast).

_____

_____

_____

_____

LAB **Group Work** Sound Waves

Question Do sound waves travel more easily through air or water?

Procedure

1. Place a water balloon against your ear. Rest a ticking watch against the other side of the balloon. Listen to the ticking.
2. Have another group member measure the distance from your ear to the watch. Record this distance below.

_____

3. Take the balloon away. Hold the watch up near your ear. Hold it the same distance from your ear as you did before (this is the distance you measured in step 2). Listen to the ticking.
4. Repeat steps 1–4 with each member of your group.
5. What did you observe? Was the ticking louder with or without the balloon?

_____

_____

> **Materials**
> * water balloons (filled)
> * meter stick
> * watch that ticks

Analysis

1. Talk about your observations with other members of your group. How did your observations **compare** with those of other people?

_____

_____

2. Did the sound of the watch ticking travel more easily through water or air?

_____

3. Particles in liquid water are closer together than particles in air. **Infer** how this helps explain what you observed.

_____

_____

_____

PHYSICAL SCIENCE Waves • LAB

Gateway to Science Workbook • Copyright © Heinle, Cengage Learning

A VOCABULARY WORDS

Fill in the chart with a definition for each word. Then use each word in a sentence.

Word	Definition	Sentence
transparent	an object you can see through	The windows in my home are transparent.
translucent		
opaque		
reflect		
refract		

B VOCABULARY IN CONTEXT

Choose words from the box to complete the paragraph.

light sources	reflect	artificial light	~~colors~~	candles	lamp
natural light	sun	absorbed	stars	refract	

Example: A prism breaks light into _____*colors*_____.

Stars, candles, lamps, and the (1) _____ all give off their own

light. They are called (2) _____. Light can be natural or artificial. A

firefly gives off (3) _____. Like the sun and (4) _____,

its light comes from nature. A flashlight is another light source. Like lamps

and (5) _____, it is a source of (6) _____, or

light that people produce. Light from a(n) (7) _____ will

(8) _____ off a mirror. If the light passes through a glass of water, it

will bend, or (9) _____. If the light hits a black surface, the light will

be taken in, or (10) _____.

📖 Student book pages 204–205

C REFLECTION AND REFRACTION

Reading Strategy *Visualizing*

Read **Reflection and Refraction** on page 204 in your student book. Then complete number 1 and number 2 below.

> **Visualizing**
> ✓ Make a picture in your mind.

1. Reflected light bounces off an object. Moonlight is an example of reflected sunlight. Visualize this in your mind and draw a picture.	2. Refracted light bends when it passes through an object. A straw that looks bent in a glass of water is an example of refracted light. Visualize this in your mind and draw a picture.

D SEEING COLORS

Reading Strategy *Making Inferences*

Read **Seeing Colors** on page 204 in your student book. Then complete the chart. Infer which types of light each object reflects and absorbs.

> **Making Inferences**
> ✓ Use what you know to make a decision.

Object	Reflects	Absorbs
green leaf	*green light*	*all other colors of light*
white coat	1.	2.
red truck	3.	4.
blue car	5.	6.
black tire	7.	8.

E **SCIENCE SKILL Interpreting Photos**

Look at the photo and answer the questions.

1. What do you see in the picture?

   _____

2. Why can the girl see her face? What is happening to the light that hits the mirror?

   _____

   _____

F **TRANSPARENT, TRANSLUCENT, OR OPAQUE?**

Pairwork

Read **Transparent, Translucent, or Opaque?** on page 205 in your student book. Then work with a partner. Think of a house. Think of examples of transparent, translucent, or opaque things in a house.

Transparent	Translucent	Opaque
windows		

G **WRITING Classifying Information**

List four natural light sources and four artificial light sources. Tell about your list in a paragraph.

_____

_____

_____

_____

LAB **Group Work** The Path of Light

Question What path does light travel?

Procedure

1. Use a ruler to draw lines between opposite corners of all 4 index cards. This should form an "X" on each card.
2. For 3 of the cards, punch a hole where the lines cross.
3. Use a small piece of the clay to stand each of the 4 index cards up on its side.
4. Line the cards up so that you can shine a flashlight through all 3 holes, onto the fourth card. See if you can get the light to shine on the center of the "X" of the fourth card.
5. How did you get the light to shine through all 3 holes onto the fourth card?

_____

_____

Materials
- 4 index cards
- ruler
- paper punch
- modeling clay
- flashlight

6. Predict what will happen if you move one punched card slightly to the side.

_____

7. Test your prediction. Observe what happens. _____

_____

_____

Analysis

1. Was the path of light curved or straight? Was the light able to go through the holes when you moved one card to the side?

_____

_____

2. **Draw a conclusion** about the path that light travels. _____

_____

_____

A VOCABULARY WORDS

Circle the word that completes each sentence.

Example: A campfire gives off electrical / (thermal) energy.

1. A candle gives off light / sound energy when it burns.

2. The energy that runs a computer is chemical / electrical energy.

3. At the top of a hill a roller coaster has potential / kinetic energy.

4. As the roller coaster moves down the hill it has potential / kinetic energy.

5. The battery in a flashlight has chemical / electrical energy.

6. When you listen to music you hear sound / thermal energy.

7. Sources of energy that can be replaced are nonrenewable / renewable.

8. The ability to do work is thermal / mechanical energy.

B VOCABULARY IN CONTEXT

Choose words from the box to complete the paragraph.

thermal energy	kinetic energy	~~mechanical energy~~
sound energy	potential energy	light energy

Example: _Mechanical energy_ is the ability to do work.

There are different kinds of energy all around you. When you turn on a

lamp it gives off (1) _____. An oven warms food with

(2) _____. (3) _____ lets you hear a song on the

radio. Two kinds of energy let us do work. Suppose you hold a ball above your

head. The ball has a lot of (4) _____. Then you drop the ball. As it

falls it has (5) _____.

C POTENTIAL AND KINETIC ENERGY

Reading Strategy *Comparing and Contrasting*

Read **Potential and Kinetic Energy** on page 208 in your student book. Then use the chart to compare and contrast potential and kinetic energy.

Comparing and Contrasting

✓ Tell how things are the same (compare).

✓ Tell how things are different (contrast).

Potential Energy	Both	Kinetic Energy
Objects can move.		

D RENEWABLE AND NONRENEWABLE ENERGY

Reading Strategy *Using Idea Maps*

Read about **Renewable and Nonrenewable Energy** on page 208 of your textbook. Then fill in the idea map with facts from the reading.

Using Idea Maps

✓ Use idea maps to show the relationships between ideas.

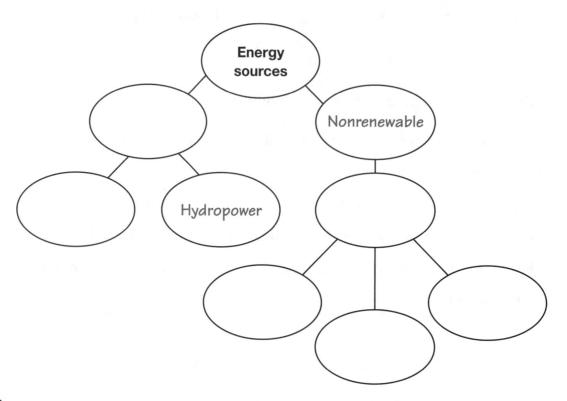

E SCIENCE SKILL Visualizing

When you visualize, you see a picture in your mind. Visualize a person on a skateboard with potential energy. Draw a picture. Then visualize the skateboarder with kinetic energy. Draw another picture.

Skateboarder with Potential Energy	Skateboarder with Kinetic Energy

F SOUND ENERGY

Pairwork

Read **Sound Energy** on page 209 in your student book. Then think of a drummer hitting a drum. How does the sound energy travel from the drum to your ear? Talk about it with a partner. Write your answer.

_____

_____

_____

G WRITING Applying Information

You are on a camping trip. You make a campfire with your parents. You cook marshmallows over the fire. What forms of energy do you see and use? Write a paragraph.

_____

_____

_____

_____

LAB **Group Work** Flashlight Energy

Question What types of energy are found in a flashlight?

Procedure

1. Take the batteries out of the flashlight. Talk with your group about how the batteries are used by the flashlight. What type of energy do you think is stored in the batteries?

Materials
• flashlight with batteries

_____

2. Place the batteries in the flashlight and turn it on. Observe what happens. Then write what type of energy you observe.

   Safety Note: Do not shine the flashlight in anyone's eyes.

_____

3. Leave the flashlight on. After 5 minutes, put your hand near the bulb of the flashlight. Discuss your observations with your group. Then, (a) write what type of energy you observe, and (b) explain how you know what type of energy it is.

   a. _____

   b. _____

4. Turn off the flashlight. Talk about your observations with your group.

Analysis

1. When the flashlight is turned off and stored in a drawer, does it have potential energy or kinetic energy? Explain your **conclusion.**

_____

2. Do other light sources give off the same types of energy as a flashlight? Give an example.

_____

_____

Gateway to Science Workbook • Copyright © Heinle, Cengage Learning

Name _____ Date _____

📖 Student book pages 210–211

A VOCABULARY WORDS

Unscramble the words to complete the sentences.

Example: thigl neygre

Fireworks give off _____light energy_____.

1. **petemrarute**

   A thermometer is used to measure _____.

2. **ellicacter neeygr**

   A toaster uses _____.

3. **mtehral neyegr**

   Fire gives off _____.

4. **iticnek ygrnee**

   _____ is energy of motion.

5. **ottpialen grneey**

   A bike at the top of a hill has _____.

B VOCABULARY IN CONTEXT

Choose words from the box to complete the paragraph.

electrical energy	light energy	sound energy	potential energy
kinetic energy	~~heat~~	thermal energy	chemical energy

Example: The movement of thermal energy is _____heat_____.

How does energy change from one form to another? Turn on the lights. A

lightbulb changes (1) _____ to (2) _____. Turn on a

CD. Electrical energy changes to (3) _____. You hear music. Hold a

ball high up in the air, then let it drop. (4) _____ changes to

(5) _____. Strike a match. Chemical energy in the match

changes to light energy and (6) _____. Use a flashlight.

(7) _____ in the battery changes to light energy.

C HEAT AND TEMPERATURE

Reading Strategy *Sequencing*

Read **Heat and Temperature** on page 212 in your student book. Then fill in the blanks with the words in the box.

> **Sequencing**
> ✓ Sequence tells you the order in which things happen.
> ✓ Words like first, next, after that, and finally can explain the sequence of something.

First	Next	After that	Finally

_____ thermal energy moves from the pan to the eggs.

_____ you put some eggs into a hot pan.

_____ the temperature of the eggs increases.

_____ the particles in the eggs move faster.

D HEATING MATTER

Reading Strategy *Facts and Examples*

Read **Heating Matter** on page 212 in your student book. As you read, write down facts in the chart about the ways thermal energy moves. Then write down one example for each fact.

> **Facts and Examples**
> ✓ Write down facts as you read.
> ✓ Write down an example for each fact.

Fact	Example
Conduction is the transfer of heat when particles bump into one another.	

Gateway to Science Workbook • Copyright © Heinle, Cengage Learning

Name _____ Date _____

E **SCIENCE SKILL** **Thinking about Systems**

Look at the picture of the toaster. Answer the questions.

> **Thinking about Systems**
> ✓ A system is made of parts that work together.

1. What are the parts of this system?

   _____

2. Where does energy come from?

   _____

3. What energy transformation takes place inside the toaster?

   _____

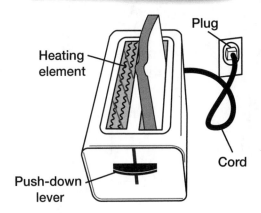

Plug

Heating element

Cord

Push-down lever

F **CONSERVATION OF ENERGY**

Pairwork

With a partner, drop and catch a tennis ball several times. Then work together to answer the questions.

1. When does the ball have only potential energy? _____

   _____

2. When does the ball have kinetic energy? _____

   _____

3. Does the total energy of the ball ever change? _____

   _____

G **WRITING** **Inferring from Evidence**

You put a cup of cold water outside on a sunny day. Later, the water feels warm. What happened? Write a paragraph. Use the words *energy, travels, thermal energy,* and *temperature* in your paragraph.

> **Inferring from Evidence**
> ✓ Make a guess about something from facts you know.

_____

_____

_____

_____

LAB **Group Work** Energy of Position

Question How does height affect potential energy?

Procedure
1. Make a stack of all 6 textbooks. Set one end of the track on the books and one end on the floor, to make a hill. Tape the track to the floor.
2. Measure the height of the stack of books. Record the height in the data table below.

Materials
- toy car
- 6 textbooks
- tagboard or foam board for track
- meter stick or tape measure
- masking tape

Books	Height of books (in centimeters)	Distance traveled (in centimeters)
6		
5		
4		
3		
2		
1		

3. Put the car at the top of the hill. Let it roll down the hill. Do not push it.
4. Measure the distance from the bottom of the track to the place where the car stopped. Use centimeters.
5. Record the distance you measured. Remove one of the books.
6. Repeat steps 2–5 five more times. Use the data table to organize your data.

Analysis
1. **Interpret your data.** What happened to the distance the car traveled as you removed books from the stack?

_____

2. How did the height of the books affect the car's energy? When did the car have the most potential energy? Write your **conclusions.**

_____

_____

_____

Name _____ Date _____

A VOCABULARY WORDS

Use the clues to fill in the crossword puzzle.

Down

1. Chlorophyll is found inside plant ____.

3. Plants make most of their food in their ____.

Across

2. ____ traps light energy from the sun.

4. The way plants use light energy to make food is called ____.

5. Sugar contains chemical ____.

6. Plants trap light energy from the ____ to make food.

B VOCABULARY IN CONTEXT

Choose words from the box to complete the paragraph.

photosynthesis	light energy	sun
cellular respiration	chemical energy	~~leaves~~

Example: Photosynthesis occurs in the _____leaves_____ of plants.

Living things need energy. You get energy from the food you eat. Energy in

food comes from the (1) _____. Plants trap (2) _____

from the sun. Plants use this energy to make food. This is called

(3) _____. The food plants make is a type of sugar. Sugar has

(4) _____. The plant stores this energy. When you eat part of

a plant, you are eating some of this stored energy. The stored energy is changed by

your body. Your body changes stored energy into energy you can use. This is called

(5) _____.

C LIVING THINGS USE THE SUN'S ENERGY

Reading Strategy *Comparing and Contrasting*

Read the paragraph. Use it to compare where plants and animals get their energy. Complete the chart.

> **Comparing and Contrasting**
> ✓ Tell how things are the same (compare).
> ✓ Tell how things are different (contrast).

The sun supplies energy for all life on Earth. Earth would be too cold for living things without the sun. The sun provides heat that seeds need to grow. These seeds grow into plants that use the sun's energy to grow and make food. People and animals cannot make their own food. They get energy by using plants for food.

Plants	Both	People and Animals
	The sun supplies energy they need.	

D PHOTOSYNTHESIS

Reading Strategy *Main Idea and Details*

Read the paragraph. Use it to complete the chart with details that support the main idea.

> **Main Idea and Details**
> ✓ The main idea of a paragraph is the big idea.
> ✓ Details support the main idea.

Plants need to make their own food. Plants use energy from the sun to make the food they need. This is called photosynthesis. Chlorophyll, the green matter found in plant leaves, traps the light energy. The plant uses this energy to combine carbon dioxide and water to make food. The food that plants make is called glucose. It is a kind of sugar. Glucose has chemical energy the plant can store.

Main Idea: Plants need to make their own food.		
Detail	**Detail**	**Detail**

E SCIENCE SKILL Making Observations

Look at the drawing of photosynthesis and read the
information. Then answer the questions.

Arrows pointing at the plant show what the
plant needs and where these things come from.
The arrow pointing away shows where oxygen goes
when it is released. The lines show where glucose is stored.

Light energy
Oxygen
Atmosphere
Glucose (chemical
energy) storage
Carbon dioxide
Water
Ground

1. What three things does the plant need for photosynthesis? _____

    _____

2. What does the plant store? What does it release? _____

    _____

F CELLULAR RESPIRATION

Pairwork

Read **Cellular Respiration** on page 217 of your student book. Look at the drawing on
the page. Discuss these questions with your partner: (1) Where do the two processes
take place? (2) What materials does each process use? (3) What are the products?

G WRITING Making Inferences

Mateo set one plant in the sunlight near the
window. He set another plant in a dark corner of the
room. That plant got only a little sunlight each day.
Tell what you think happened to the plants. Write a
paragraph.

_____

_____

_____

_____

LAB **Group Work** Respiration

Question What does yeast need to grow?

Procedure

1. Use masking tape and a marking pen to number and label the plastic bottles. Label them bottle 1 and bottle 2.
2. Fill each bottle half full of warm water. Add 1 spoonful of sugar to bottle 1. Observe both bottles and record your observations below.

   Bottle 1: _____

   Bottle 2: _____

3. Add 1 spoonful of yeast to each bottle. Put the lids on the bottles. Gently shake each bottle to mix the contents. Remove the lids from the bottles.
4. Every 5 minutes, observe any changes that happen in the bottles. Record your observations in the chart.

Materials
- warm water
- sugar
- marker
- fast-acting yeast
- 2 plastic spoons
- clock or watch
- 2 clean plastic bottles with lids
- masking tape

Time	Bottle 1	Bottle 2
5 minutes		
10 minutes		
15 minutes		

Analysis

1. What changes did you **observe** in each bottle? _____

   _____

   _____

2. What do you think caused the differences you observed? Write your **conclusion**.

   _____

   _____

   _____

Name _____ Date _____

A VOCABULARY WORDS

Circle the word or words that complete each sentence.

Example: A magnet has a magnetic pole / (magnetic field) around it.

1. Static electricity / Electric current can jump from place to place.

2. Static electricity / Electric current flows along a path.

3. A magnetic field is stronger / weaker at its poles.

4. Copper wire is a(n) insulator / conductor.

5. Plastic is a(n) insulator / conductor.

6. An electric current / electromagnet makes a magnetic field using electricity.

B VOCABULARY IN CONTEXT

Choose words from the box to complete the paragraph.

charge	electrons	~~electric current~~	static electricity
magnetic field	magnetic poles	circuit	electromagnet

Example: Metal wires spin inside a magnetic field to make ___electric current___.

When (1) _____ move between atoms, an electric

(2) _____ is formed. Rub a balloon on a cat's fur. The fur will

stand up and stick to the balloon. This is because of an electric charge called

(3) _____. Electric current is another kind of electric charge. It flows

along a path called a(n) (4) _____. You can use electric current to

make a(n) (5) _____. Like all magnets, this kind of magnet has a(n)

(6) _____ and two (7) _____.

📖 Student book pages 220–221

C STATIC AND CURRENT ELECTRICITY

Reading Strategy *Comparing and Contrasting*

Read **Static and Current Electricity** on page 220 of your student book. Then fill in the Venn diagram.

> **Comparing and Contrasting**
> ✓ Tell how things are the same (compare).
> ✓ Tell how things are different (contrast).

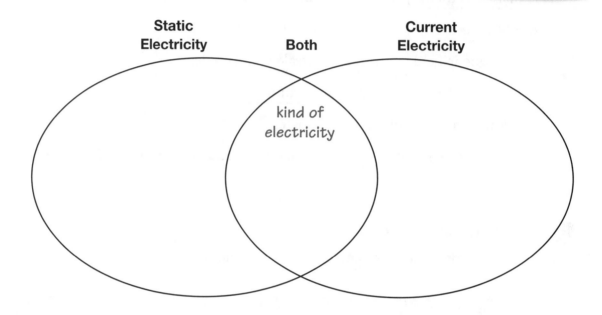

Static Electricity   Both   Current Electricity

kind of electricity

D CIRCUITS

Reading Strategy *Cause and Effect*

Read **Circuits** on page 220 of your student book. Then answer the questions.

> **Cause and Effect**
> ✓ The cause tells what happened.
> ✓ The effect is the result of the cause.

1. *Cause:* A switch opens the circuit.

   Effect: What happens to the light?

   _____

2. *Effect:* The light goes on.

   Cause: What causes the light to go on?

   _____

E SCIENCE SKILL Reading a Circuit Diagram

Look at the circuit diagram below. Then answer the questions.

1. How many batteries are part of this circuit? How many lightbulbs?

   _____

2. Are the lights on or off? How do you know?

   _____

   _____

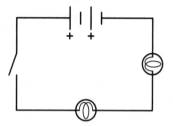

F CONDUCTORS AND INSULATORS

Pairwork

Work with a partner. Read **Conductors and Insulators** on page 221 of your student book. Then answer the questions.

1. Why is electrical wire often made of copper? _____

   _____

2. Why is electrical wire often covered in plastic? _____

   _____

3. What do you think you should do if you see bare electrical wires? _____

   _____

G WRITING Integrating Information

You pull clothes out of a dryer. Some socks are stuck together. You pull them apart and get a small static shock. Explain what happened. Use the words *electrons, positive, negative, gained,* and *lost* in your paragraph.

_____

_____

_____

_____

_____

LAB Group Work Make an Electromagnet

Question How does electricity change a nail?

Procedure

1. Make a small pile of paper clips on the table. Touch them with the iron nail. What happens?

   _____

2. Wrap the wire around the nail. The wire should form a coil or spiral around the nail. Leave 15–20 centimeters of wire at each end.
3. Tape one end of the wire to one end of the battery.
4. Tape the other end of the wire to the other end of the battery.
5. Touch the paper clips with the nail. What happens?

   _____

Materials
- copper wire
- iron nail
- D battery
- paper clips
- masking tape

Analysis

1. **Draw a conclusion** about how electricity changed the nail.

   _____

2. Suppose you added another battery to the electromagnet. **Predict** what would happen.

   _____

   _____